Angel Chairs:
New Work by Wendell Castle

Angel Chairs:
New Work by Wendell Castle

Angel Chairs:
New Work by Wendell Castle

Essays by
Arthur C. Danto
Peter T. Joseph and Emma T. Cobb

Peter Joseph Gallery
New York 1991

Photography by Michael Galatis

Design by Michael Bierut/Pentagram

Drawings by Wendell Castle

Production by Lorry Parks Dudley

Library of Congress Catalog Card Number: 91-060156

ISBN: 0-9628849-0-1

Contents

Acknowledgments

Peter T. Joseph

any people have helped me along the path that led to the opening of the Peter Joseph Gallery. Warren and Bebe Johnson first introduced me to the field of studio furniture. Through their gallery, Pritam & Eames, they guided me in assembling the collection with which I have lived so happily for the past nine years. John Dunnigan first suggested the idea of a Manhattan gallery devoted to studio furniture. With his urging and support, supplemented by that of Richard Newman, I seriously began to consider the endeavor.

The idea took on more energy when I started working with Wendell Castle and Lorry Parks Dudley. Lorry introduced me to Albert Paley, Sydney and Frances Lewis, Davira Taragin and others who offered encouragement, advice and inspiration. Lorry's introduction to Michael Galatis proved wonderfully propitious. He is responsible for the fine photography displayed in these pages. Without the confidence I have come to have in Lorry, and without the trust that goes with the friendship we have developed, I would not have gone ahead with the Gallery. The Gallery may bear my name, but her hard work has made it all possible. She will be its Director and will be the person responsible for making it work day to day.

Wendell Castle and Lorry Dudley join me in thanking those who have worked so hard and so skillfully helping to make the pieces for this show: Connie Ayres, Lucien Casartelli, Peggy Fleming, Deanna Funk, David Fowler, Greg Johnson, Peter Klingensmith, John Krenzer, Aminta Romaguera, Brian Rooney, Bill Sellers, Bill Sloane, Don Sottile, Jeff Webster, Glenn Winters and Scott Zupp. Nancy Jurs, of course, deserves a special note of gratitude.

The Delaware Art Museum, Charles Dailey, and Sydney and Frances Lewis have been kind enough to loan work for this show.

Emma Cobb collaborated with me in writing "Itty Bitty Tables and Apocalyptic Chairs." Her careful observations and imaginative insight have helped me see and understand Wendell Castle's art better than I had before.

Many others have helped with the Gallery and have earned my gratitude: Cynthia Beck, for her helping hand in the preliminary stages; Patricia Conway and Jack Lenor Larsen, for their support and encouragement; Peter Zweig, with assistance from Margaret Sobieski, Alan Gordon, and Clark Construction, for the design and construction of the space; Steven Simkin and Colleen Codey of Paul, Weiss, Rifkind, Wharton & Garrison, and Susan Levy of LaSalle Partners, who worked together to foreshorten the usual agony of a lease negotiation; Michael Bierut, for his help with all of our graphic design needs, including this catalogue; and Frances Gerngross and Carole Hochman, for their enthusiasm, support, and advice. Also, I say thank you to Jim Giangrasso, VanBuren N. Hansford, Jr., Nancy Higginbottom, Michael Montayer, John Silberman and Eileen Silvers.

Among those who deserve special thanks are all of my colleagues at Rosecliff. Their curiosity, tolerance, and general good humor have enabled me to embark on this project. I must single out Kathy Duffin, who has always been there when I needed her, with her warm manner, sound judgment and friendship.

It goes without saying that the artists who have joined me at the Peter Joseph Gallery will be its lifeblood. I commit to them that I will do my part, but ultimately our success will ride on their work. So, to all of the artists—James Carpenter, Wendell Castle, John Dunnigan, Michelle Holzapfel, Thomas Hucker, Michael Hurwitz, Wendy Maruyama, Alphonse Mattia, Richard Scott Newman, Albert Paley, Gaetano Pesce, Timothy Philbrick, Rosanne Somerson, Wendy Stayman and Ed Zucca—I say thank you for rising to the challenge.

Finally, I thank Wendy Evans for her friendship and for our time together.

Furniture: Our Chosen Canvas

t is the mission of the Peter Joseph Gallery to traverse the gulf that separates art from furniture. However they may be classified, the objects here displayed will represent the highest level of creative expression. Some will reflect devotion to craftsmanship or to a particular tradition of furniture-making; others may resist or radically reinterpret the established order. Whatever approach they embody, the best will become the furniture masterpieces of this century and, as such, will be passed down from generation to generation. A few, like the great furniture pieces of the past, will be destined for museums; but in truth, their proper domain is the home.

A home filled with furniture is a portrait in collage that we make of and for ourselves. Furniture helps us through the everyday patter of our lives. We sleep in beds, we sit in chairs, we eat at tables, we work at desks. We define ourselves through our furniture; and it, in turn, speaks to us about our world, reflecting not only our own dreams and aspirations but also those of our culture. As our most constant companion, furniture is a source of reflection, meditation, and inspiration.

Ordinary furniture is inherently con-servative. It is designed and manufactured to meet, not challenge, expectations; to reflect the times rather than to comment on them; to comfort us rather than provoke us. Such furniture invariably becomes a symbol of its age. Consider, for example, the despotic excesses embalmed in Tutankhamen's lavish throne; or the couches on which citizens of ancient Athens lay, their confident idealism tak-ing supine form; or massive, Gothic trestle tables freighted with the rigid spirituality and brutal appetites of their Dark Age; or the gilt and tendrilled pieces on which the aristocracy of Louis XVI perched and teetered, soon to fall; or the smooth, steel tubing of an International Style chair, offering cold comfort to a civilization being transformed by industry; or the molded, standardized seating that gratified

America's conformist longings after World War II.

Art furniture, on the other hand, is intentionally provocative. It enters our lives on an especially profound level. By compelling us to reflect on deeply ingrained, often unconscious, habits of seeing and use, it sometimes confounds us. By offering new insights into ourselves and our culture, and by opening up unforeseen possibilities, it inspires us. As Arthur Danto observes, art furniture provides metaphors by which we can better understand the way we live.

The works of art furniture shown in this Gallery will express highly personal and diverse visions. John Dunnigan's generously proportioned paeans to Biedermeier have a surprising grace, and his richly textured fabrics embellish those historicizing themes. With his witty, anthropomorphic valets, Alphonse Mattia imaginatively explores the foibles of self-presentation. Wendy Maruyama plays primitive imagery against a rectilinear style, warmed by a palette of tropical exuberance. Layers of sculptural detail within symmetrical frames give a brooding depth to Rosanne Somerson's tables and chairs. The pale, slender-limbed furniture that Michael Hurwitz makes has an Oriental purity and reserve. Thomas Hucker's work embodies a similarly austere, Japanese aesthetic, but with darker meditative concerns. Richard Scott Newman brings a reverence for wood to his meticulously executed studies in a neoclassical mode. Of a more flamboyant temper, Edward Zucca's sculpted images carry vivid political messages, as do Wendell Castle's coy subversions of the material order. The sinuous objects Albert Paley coaxes out of steel movingly belie their compact, natural power. And Gaetano Pesce's urethane chairs give us occasion to reflect, once again, on the extraordinary iconic power of that simple form.

The keystone of the distinction so often made between art and furniture is function. The former is useless, the latter is useful—or so it is said. When utility becomes a consideration, other valued concerns—concerns praised as aesthetic—receive correspondingly short shrift. Even if accepted as a creative issue in its own right, function is deemed to be somehow less worthy than others.

Why is function so condemned? That it constitutes a constraint cannot alone account for the stigma. Any artist confronts and responds to innumerable constraints, whether by reaffirming or contradicting them. There is no particular reason why function, as one aspect of what both we and the artist understand about a work of art, should compromise, rather than enhance, its aesthetic virtues. Why, indeed, should function itself not count as such a virtue?

In fact, functional requirements can be and always have been among the most fruitful and stimulating challenges to the creative impulse. The perception of function not only advances the meaning of a work, but it also broadens the scope and intensity of what can be communicated. When the function in question belongs to furniture, the meaning comes home to us in a particularly profound and literal way.

Art furniture, precisely because of its functionality, thus insinuates itself into our daily lives more deeply and pervasively than many of the so-called fine arts. Like architecture, that other medium of the built world, furniture engages us in very subliminal ways. Even more than the architect, an artist who speaks through furniture is sure to be persistently and powerfully heard, for his voice is more personal and intimate. It speaks from the interiors of our homes rather than merely from the houses that they fill.

Many artists working within the sculptural tradition have understood and explored the great communicative power that furniture has. Foremost among them is the late Scott Burton, whose *Bronze Chair* (1972/75) has become an emblem of the debate percolating at the borders of the art and furniture worlds. The piece, a Queen-

Anne style chair cast in bronze, is an exemplar of the very
sort of ambiguity that the debaters seek to resolve. The
piece has the material patina of art, but it is also fully ser-
viceable as a chair. It may be a bit heavy to move, and a bit
hard for prolonged sitting, but in every sense of the word it
is a chair—unless its very success as sculpture inescapably,
and inexplicably, defeats its character as furniture.

Burton sought out furniture as his
language because he understood furniture's special ability to
convey meaning. His ambition was to mount his message
on work that was useful—and thereby to reach what he
called the democratic, non-elite, non-art audience. He
wanted to take the Minimalist form that had so influenced
him and make it talk. Furniture was his chosen canvas.

Useful or not, the works to be shown
here neither call for nor invite classification, whether as
furniture or as art. Their unequivocal success in no way
hangs on such a judgment; for they are, *at once,* both. Their
achievement resides, instead, in the extraordinary intelligence, imagination, and skill that goes into their making,
and in the meaning that they carry. It is the Peter Joseph
Gallery's great privilege and pleasure to permit these works
to speak, at last, for themselves.

February 1991

II

"Out of the Corner of My Eye"

Wendell Castle

A lot of what happens in my work is a kind of magic. I say that partly because I don't really understand what's going on much of the time. When I sketch, which is often, I very consciously try not to judge or edit. I never erase, even if a line really goes astray or gets a big wiggle in it. That wiggle and that wrong line may turn out to be the right line.

Creativity is exploration. It helps to know what you're looking for, so you'll know whether or not you've found it. But along the way, while you're looking, it's better not to head just for that one thing. Let yourself go off on a tangent or be distracted by other activities, because you may find something far more wonderful than what you were actually looking for. I might have a deadline to design a desk, for instance, and be drawing away, when suddenly my drawing will look a lot more like a chair than a desk. So there I'll be, designing chairs, and tomorrow I'll still have a deadline for a desk.

Frequently I ask myself, "What if?" What if I took away this or added that? What if I turned it upside down? What if I did something crazy? What if the legs to a table went up to the ceiling instead of down to the floor? I made a dining room table where exactly that happened. What if some of the legs went to the floor and some of them went to the wall? I tried that as well. What if a piece of furniture had fifteen or twenty legs? What if it had only one leg? What if the hierarchy of furniture parts were turned upside down, so that the tops of tables became smaller and the legs became bigger? What if a cabinet rocked?

I never try to solve a problem by facing it. I sneak up on it, or put it on a mental back-burner. I walk into my studio at night without turning on the lights so that I can look at pieces in very poor light. I walk by a piece and look at it out of the corner of my eye. Sometimes if you square right up to a piece, just walk up to it and try to solve a problem, you're not going to succeed.

So I sneak up on a piece. I look at it out of the corner of my eye, or turn it upside down in the shop for a few days.

When the pieces are on saw horses in the shop, they're always upside down or on their sides. I saw one of the wing shapes on its side one day and thought it could rock, so I turned it into a rocker. The wings in another piece change completely; they are transformed into legs, and the piece becomes a desk. I was trying to develop a body of chairs, and all of a sudden I had a desk.

At the beginning I felt like an explorer staking out new territory. Each work was another fence post defining the terrain. I needed a lot of fence posts.

In the early 1960s, my assistants sanded. Sanding took up 25 to 30 percent of the time required to build one of my organic pieces. Then my vocabulary changed; by the late 1970s, cabinetmaking had become a time-consuming part of my work, and I wanted help. For the first time, I added true cabinetmakers to my studio. This meant I had to calculate all aspects of a piece very carefully in advance, leaving little to chance, so I could make drawings that someone else could understand well enough to build the piece. Without realizing it, I was gradually turning into a designer to accommodate the extraordinarily talented people I had with me. In a way, it was easier in the early days. I had no commissions, no deadlines, not much help and no restrictions of any kind. I had only myself to please.

With the warped-top table series, I switched back to what is most important to me: change, risk, learning from the work, not predetermining every-thing. My assistants now allow me to do the parts that challenge me most. They keep the work moving so that learning will be at its highest.

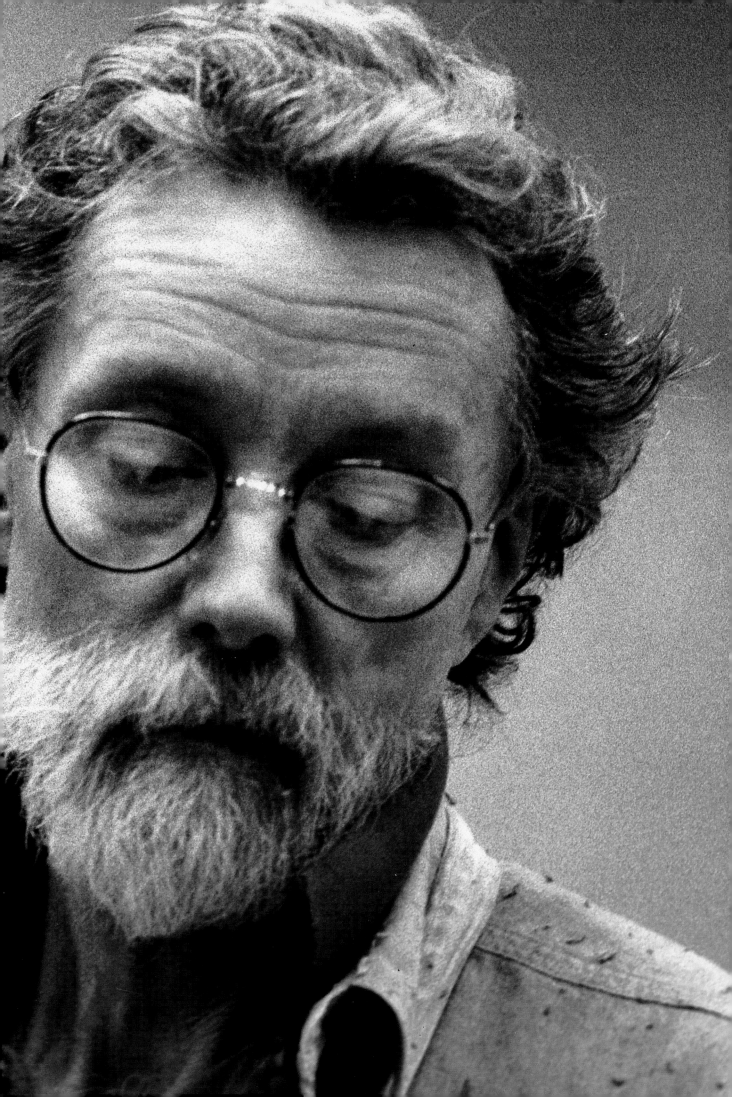

Itty Bitty Tables and Apocalyptic Chairs

Peter T. Joseph
and
Emma T. Cobb

eave it to Wendell Castle to discover the neglected potential in any object. He has been doing so quite brilliantly for thirty years. With his Pedestal Pieces and Angel Chairs, the two groups of works featured here, he succeeds once again.

Pedestals and chairs would seem to have little in common. Both shoulder burdens; but there the resemblance surely ends. Unless we feel capable of sitting, like Saint Simeon, on top of a column for thirty years, we are unlikely to see the pedestal as fit for human occupation. Nor, conversely, is it in the nature of the chair to point itself towards heaven in an act of self-conscious display; that is a pedestal's perogative.

Castle's chairs, however, are no mere carriers of the mortal frame. They resist the earthbound limitations of the ordinary seat by sprouting an impressive pair of wings. Likewise, his pedestals live down a legacy of mute service on behalf of thankless things. They are unmistakably occupied, if not by actual persons, by authentic personalities.

The artist's prodigious output has included cabinets, clocks, lamps, walls, humidors and stairs, as well as those quintessential furnishings, tables and chairs. Like any expanding universe, Castle's has become less restricted—and less predictable—as he has traveled further from its core. Though his work has always declared its freedom from furniture-like constraints, his latest pieces transcend that struggle in an extraordinary way.

Castle is a master of the polar extreme; in the past, he has chosen to cultivate such extremes one at a time. At various moments in his career, he has experimented with a highly organic style, generating plant-like seats and peanut-shaped chests; with an intense, historical formalism calling for inlays of more than eight thousand dots and upholstery on the bottoms of chairs; with astonishing feats of trompe l'oeil; and with exotically hued studies of geometric volume.

Scribe Stool
1960

Castle's current work draws spectacularly on all of this imagery. Wood is juxtaposed to metal, rough surfaces to smooth, organic forms to crisply volumetric ones. More than Castle's previous work, so often devoted to the singular effect, these pieces describe a new and complicated realm. We are less inclined to ask what they are—plant or plane? sculpture or furniture?—than who.

The joint appearance of pedestals and chairs in itself represents a marriage of the old and new. The chair was Castle's very first piece of furniture; while the pedestal is an ultimate refinement of the table, the form that has absorbed most of his attention during the last three decades. The Pedestal Pieces and the Angel Chairs constitute nothing less than a rebirth for both furniture forms. It is hardly the first such event in Wendell Castle's career; many similar metamorphoses preceded the one that takes place here. The story of that evolution is a fundamental part of what these pieces are, and deserves telling.

Castle's first foray into furniture as a sculptural subject produced a version of the oldest furnishing in the world: the stool. Primitive though they are, Castle's *Stool Sculpture* (1959) and *Scribe Stool* (1960) express the same iconoclasm towards the convention of platform and base that his later work so brazenly displays.

Castle calls *Scribe Stool* a "high chair for adults." The description embodies an oxymoron of the sort the artist loves. High chairs are for children. For adults they are an absurdity, ambiguously comical and disturbing. As a practical arrangement, the merging of table and seat into a single unit undermines the functional distinctions between those surfaces. That monolithic image appears frequently throughout Castle's work of the 1960s, and reflects his burgeoning interest in furniture's supporting elements—its base or its legs.

Like much of the work to follow,

Scribe Stool is made of laminated wood, carved to an organic taper and swell. The piece has the branching delicacy of bones and roots, but its overall effect is distinctly tree-like. The shadowy emergence of its namesake from the upper branches has a bewildering strangeness. It is as if the high chair had been prematurely frozen, abandoned halfway through a Daphne-like transformation into a tree.

The concentration of crisscrossing limbs accentuates the stool's freedom from practical obligations. The five tapering branches slope up from the ground towards the center, but each branch then pulls away, engaging the others in an overlapping cross that dimly evokes the x-shaped stretcher of a chair. The energy of the piece is all down below, along with a signature Castle touch: feet of startling slimness and delicacy. Any support these so-called legs begrudge the stool is ambivalent and indirect; this object surrenders no part of itself to what utility might demand.

Castle eventually advanced to the table. Unshackled from its traditional constraints, the table has been a powerful ally in Castle's campaign to free furniture from its legacy of servitude. *Wall Table No. 16* (1969), carved out of stack-laminated afrormosia, is an early crusader in that cause. This ambitious object extends one of two trunk-like appendages to the wall, where the face of the table's cylindrical section meets the surface with what looks like a vacuum-tight grip. The other elephantine member dips to the floor and hugs it with equal tenacity. Along the way, a horizontal plane occurs. It looks almost accidental, as if the hump of an otherwise continuous, curving tube had been sliced off. An elevated platform is, to be sure, part of what this table offers; yet one is not even tempted to look to that platform for this object's essential being. The table has been liberated from what its maker believes to be the cruelest of dogmas: that it was born primarily to serve.

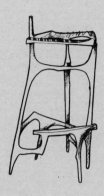

Wall Table behaves as if its body were entirely its own, refusing to distinguish among any of the surfaces external to it. It gives no special privilege, for example, to the floor, finding the wall to be as adequate a resting place as any. Not only does this "table" consist almost entirely of leg, but that leg has literally risen above what might, in ordinary circumstances, have been considered a table's primary achievement and reason to be: the tabletop.

In *Cloth Without Table* (1979), Castle conjures up an elevated surface with no legs at all. The piece is one of the finer products of the artist's passing infatuation with trompe l'oeil. Drapery carved out of laminated cherry appears to cover and hang down from a small table; the illusion of fabric is intensified by the exposed lamination, which creates a pattern that follows the sculpted folds. The table itself–that four-cornered, elevated platform so uncannily insinuated to lie beneath the surface–is entirely absent. No tapered feet peep out from under the carved-on hem. The imitation cloth stands rigidly alone, suspending itself on one side by meeting the floor in a sprawl. Like a magician's veil, the piece stages the disappearance of an object that was never there at all.

If *Wall Table* had territorial designs on the wall, *Cloth Without Table* wants to own the floor. The "cloth" is already overabundant; even properly adjusted, it would engulf the hypothesized piece of furniture. There is something disreputable, even decadent, in such material largesse, and in the wanton carelessness with which the fabric drifts to one side and begins its slide across the floor. The scene hints of the boudoir or the bordello. While the earthly body of the piece may be entirely absent, its corporeal character lingers on, like perfume.

Cloth Without Table withholds not only the expected form–the table itself–but in so doing it also withdraws the whole idea of that form's function. Self-

elimination is the supreme achievement of the piece. It is no mere magician's handkerchief we witness here, but Houdini himself, in the middle of the act.

In *Ghost Clock* (1985), that same obliterative impulse, apparently unappeased, extends to other things as well. The furniture missing from *Cloth Without Table* is ostensibly present here, only to disappear under a suffocating embrace. A grandfather clock, ordinarily quite anthropoid, looks more so cloaked. This phantom timepiece seems as helpless as a dress form inside its primly cinched bedsheet. The spectacle is that of an aged patriarch, heartlessly silenced and bound for eternity with a scrap of knotted string.

Clock, covering, and string are carved out of mahogany, stained and bleached to a remarkable verisimilitude. The trick is almost too good; but this is precisely why *Ghost Clock,* the last of Castle's major trompe l'oeil efforts, makes such a fitting coda to the series. Castle's boredom with the style was in part the product of his thorough mastery of it. With the exception of *Cloth Without Table* and *Ghost Clock,* two works in which the illusory effect advances a more complex statement, the trompe l'oeil works have but a single tale to tell. The genre makes an art of the first and second glance; after that, there is no more.

Demilune Table (1981), in contrast, cultivates the long and penetrating gaze. The work typifies Castle's reaction to the privations, aesthetic and otherwise, of his trompe l'oeil endeavors. Having immersed himself in the period styles that served both as subjects and as props for his illusions, Castle allied himself to principles antithetical to illusionism. The latter succeeds by persuading us to overlook detail. *Demilune Table,* in all its richness, invites the deepest scrutiny we can muster.

The inspiration for this contemplative undertaking was the French Art Deco designer Emile-

Wall Table No. 16
1969

Jacques Ruhlmann, considered by many to be the last of the great *ébénistes*. Though not a cabinetmaker himself, Ruhlmann scrupulously supervised every stage of the execution of his designs. His exacting standards were anomalous in an age when careless mass-production was increasingly the rule. Such perfectionism was more typical of eighteenth-century master craftsmen, whose principles Ruhlmann revered and imitated. Like the masters' cabinetry, Ruhlmann's called for the finest materials and flawless, labor-intensive execution. The cost was correspondingly great, but it was willingly borne by the wealthy Parisian clientele that Ruhlmann had so shrewdly cultivated. The calculated splendor of those rarefied lives is mirrored in every piece of furniture that Ruhlmann made.

In a virtuoso display of all of these qualities, *Demilune Table* pays homage to the Ruhlmann style. (Castle's 1981 *Lady's Desk with Two Chairs* is a better-known example of his Ruhlmannian fervor.) The tabletop—actually half of a dodecagon—features a fiery, Brazilian-rosewood veneer laid in six triangular panels that create a dark sunburst pattern. The surface is recessed from the bulk of the top, which develops an almost cylindrical swell around the edges as it descends. It is massive compared to the four attenuated legs. Gracefully rectilinear and slightly tapered, they are set into the outer edge of the top, rising just above it. The face of each leg is outlined with an inlay of tiny ivory dots; a similar inlay traces the perimeter of the tabletop. Finally, four carved-ivory lozenges, actually elongated demilunes, stand up from the tops of the legs. Smaller ivory pastilles serve as feet of exaggerated delicacy, but the superior elements are the more powerful presence in this piece. These ivory pennants are extravagant baubles; yet their superfluity is hardly apparent, so smoothly are they absorbed into the concentrated discipline—even austerity—of the table's overall design.

In evoking an upper reach of privi-leged domesticity, this table belongs to a realm where no amount of skill or labor comes at a price too high. The table's meticulous execution, the seamlessness of its detail, embody a real resource of power as well as an aesthetic ideal. The table tells no more of the actual hands that made it than does a piece of haute couture; like such a garment, it reflects only its real or imagined possessors.

The intense and brooding formalism of *Demilune Table* had inevitably to give way to the realities it denied; to disorder where there was order; to floating fragments where there once was a whole. *Demilune Table* is dominated by powerful but self-contained ideals; in *Dr. Caligari's Desk and Chair* (1986), that authoritarian impulse runs amok with its own malign visions. The piece depicts the virtual breaking down of a world.

The tableau, inspired by the sets of the 1919 German expressionist film *Das Kabinett des Dr. Caligari,* has all the stark abruptness of the early cinema. Every surface is a jagged polygon; the units are glaringly whitewashed and streaked with violent, painted wisps of black and gray. In the vocabulary of the moving image, these flourishes connote desperate haste and explosive power, but the desk and chair ultimately belong to a static pictorial reality. They look like sketches made three-dimensional.

The ensemble memorializes a tale of insanity and devious persecution, evoking a world in which fantasy and reality have ceased to be separate realms. The desk and chair are the furniture of a hallucinatory nightmare; even the drawer pulls have a chilling presence. Lodged in the concave angle of each drawer, the four silver-plated steel eyelets extend out to a menacing distance. The long rods penetrate the drawers at their weakest point, seeming to make the entire unit buckle even further. They hint of the dungeon or the torture chamber, or—perhaps worst of all—the operating room. They are surely the instruments of some

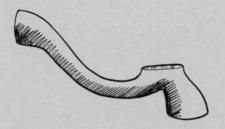

unsavory and highly unorthodox procedure.

At the bottom of the drawer unit, an even strip of ebonized cherry constitutes an isolated instance of order. The gesture seems designed to seal off or contain the frenzy overhead; a sketched imitation of this effort reappears at the base of the chair. The slick, black platform, like a Kommandant's polished boot, manifests either the obsessive propriety of the insane or the dapper efficiency of genuine evil.

The question is precisely what the nature of this vision is. Is it a paranoid fantasy, or the reflection of some real, persecutory hazard in the world? The history of *Das Kabinett des Dr. Caligari* suggests the fragility of any answer we might give. In the original version of the film, Dr. Caligari, a psychiatrist, is an authoritarian monster who destroys the sanity and will of his helpless patient. In the later version edited by the German government, a kindly Dr. Caligari attempts to cure his charge of what the film now construes as mere delusions. *Dr. Caligari's Desk and Chair* leaves us at a similar impasse. What remains certain, however we receive these pieces, is that the malignancy and disorder of which they speak are enduring possibilities.

The Caligarian desk suggests a maniacal industriousness, one fraught with conflicts so severe that productivity is virtually paralyzed. The powerful compulsion to work and control must vie against almost overwhelming turmoil. In a parallel fashion, *Dr. Caligari's Library* (1987-8) offers its interpretation of the activity a library ideally implies. The life of the mind is again the subject; study and contemplation are the external orders that are shown to mask the chaos and anarchy within.

There are, to begin with, no identifiable, unitary walls here, only fragments, or boundaries between fragments. A black, leatherbound shelf separates a series of gessoed panels above from a puzzle of carved and buffed satinwood pieces below. The shelf, indifferent to its

duties, rises and falls as it winds its way around the room. The abstract configuration of satinwood polygons is as porous and ethereal as a Louise Nevelson chapel. Above the shelf, trapezoidal panels of pale gesso (with bold, basic colors peeking through its white, wirebrushed surface) alternate with bookshelves knocked askew. Large doughnut shapes emerge from the gesso in high relief, some having been quartered and then haphazardly put back together again. These rings and their reassembled fragments look larger than life; like enormous corpuscles, they seem to be rising towards the surface of some unspecified fluid.

The hierarchical conventions that are allowed to drift untethered in the *Library* are transcended altogether in Castle's warped-top table series, a group of about twenty pieces produced between 1986 and 1988. *The Music Of Rubber Bands* (1986), one of the first and most important of the warped-tops, finally gains for the table the freedom it had struggled for since *Wall Table*. Up until this point, Castle had sought to overcome the limitations of the tabletop by diminishing the surface or otherwise undermining its function. In *The Music of Rubber Bands,* the tabletop is flamboyantly reborn as a voluptuous curve. Clean lacewood veneer covers both the piece's top and legs, the latter being two triangular elements that meet the floor on tiptoe. A pair of sinuous stretchers of ebonized cherry link but do not bother to brace the legs, seeming to pass through each one merely to dangle idly on its other side.

In its graphic simplicity and plastic comportment, the piece could have bounced right out of a Betty Boop cartoon. The reality to which the table belongs has all the heady freedom of a comic strip. Unbound by the compulsion to serve, to stand up straight, to be anything but itself, this perambulatory table is a free agent. There are no frightening perversions of a prescribed order here, but instead another order altogether.

The warped-top tables augured a new

Cloth Without Table

1979

freedom for Wendell Castle. They do not carry their grudges as obviously as do their predecessors; indeed, they do not carry, or need to carry, anything at all. This is not merely because, like many of Castle's tables, they preempt actual use. Whether they do or not is precisely not their concern. These tables are no longer bent, so to speak, on defining themselves in terms of what they are not. Their identities reside more in the logic of their own composition than in any of the properties they explicitly disavow. They have come into their own as autonomous objects.

Pity the Table

In the hierarchy of built objects, the table occupies a position well down on the scale of passive servitude. A table is supposed to offer elevation and support; that is conceived to be its nature, its essential identity. Surface appearance and material constitution are held to be mere accidents of time and place. So, at any rate, would a dogmatist have it.

Against this Platonic view of furniture comes the way of seeing urged on us by Wendell Castle, or rather induced by certain objects from his hand. The very idea of the unalterable tableness of tables offends him. Such a doctrine represents, to his mind, the height of insensitivity to the full range of possibilities. Castle may not yet have delivered us completely from our deepest illusions about the Table Ideal, but he comes close with the warped-tops, and closer still with his recent Pedestal Pieces.

The pedestal would seem to be the purest form of table there is. As Castle himself observes, pedestals are simply tables with itty bitty tops. Pedestals constitute the lowest common denominator of all tables, exhibiting the fundamental characteristics of elevation and support, but little else. Yet while a table can still claim some independence from the objects it carries, the pedestal

seems to relinquish not just a portion, but the whole of its autonomy. Its status is one of utter subjugation, of an object identified wholly with respect to something superior to it.

Like all of the artist's most successful works, his pedestals simultaneously demonstrate and undermine the hierarchies we habitually look for and build into our lives. The pedestal turns out to have an elusive and unexpectedly complex identity, displaying more talents than the conventional view of its essential function might suggest.

Constantin Brancusi, a sculptor whose influence permeates Castle's early stack-laminates, was similarly preoccupied with the nature and form of the pedestal. At least some of Brancusi's sculpture bases were built and conceived of as independent works, and may even have been displayed apart from any objects they were designed to bear. Castle's pedestals resemble these austere meditations in that they, too, declare the independence of the quintessentially subordinate object.

Brancusi's freestanding pedestals, like his renditions of tables and chairs, explore the sculptural quality of a functional form and demonstrate its power to ritualize as well as domesticate a given space. They also dwell on the relationship and shared identity of sculpture and base. Castle explores similar ideas; but his pedestals take as their subject what is already an adaptation of the sculptural tradition, namely, the pedestal as household object. Castle's meditations relate to objects of a particularly intimate and functional kind. The mood of such meditations may, of course, be anything but domestic.

Elevation—the principle that the pedestal so purely and unambiguously is supposed to embody— is so familiar and universal a metaphor for superiority of any kind that we are barely conscious of it. Its concrete expressions abound. What we value and wish to protect, we raise up, whether to the level of our human hands and eyes,

in the daily domestic round, or to the higher purview of the gods. Conversely, whatever is elevated invites respect, or at least due consideration of its implied merits. What we look for and find in an object is always in part what we are directed to find. The pedestal, like the picture frame, issues very powerful commands. It establishes relative worth in an instant, creating a field of veneration around its elevated charge.

What happens, then, when an ordinary bowl is taken out of the kitchen cupboard and put on the mantelpiece? What if that bowl is moved from the mantelpiece to the top of a plaster post in the corner? Here is where elevation in general, and the pedestal in particular, truly come into their own as stamps of value, as makers of household gods and kings. This is home, the place where Wendell Castle finds the subject and the language of his art. His pedestals embody more than just the universal properties of their type. They depict the pedestal as potential citizen—both lawmaker and judge—of the domestic domain.

Unlike a museum, a private dwelling does not by definition constrain us to accept, or even to consider, its contents as objects of aesthetic contemplation. In a domestic setting, elevation and isolation of any kind make a correspondingly more powerful statement. Within this peculiarly sensitized realm, the pedestal joins a second, larger class of objects that exist on the periphery. Hall tables, console tables, wall sconces, whatnots—these pieces ostensibly provide support and elevation, but more often than not they remain unburdened. Posted in corners and near doorways, these pieces have an almost ceremonial presence; they evoke, but do not necessarily invite, actual use. They add a layer of imagined domesticity to the actual scene, reflecting, but not quite participating in, the life at hand. While occasionally they do provide elevation for objects on display, in their more general function they resemble picture frames as much as pedestals.

Among the furniture population, then, hall tables and their ilk are the natural geniuses, unconscious keepers of the faith in a higher domestic reality. It is highly fitting that Castle, philosopher of the living room par excellence, should eventually have turned to the pedestal, a form embodying those principles even more purely and exclusively.

Castle's Pedestal Pieces are monopodal structures that provide elevation and support—eminently pedestal-like properties. But what do or could these structures carry? Is that cone affixed to an otherwise unobstructed, planar surface itself on display, or is it just a decorative appendage of the pedestal-support? Or what about the proud elevation, in another piece, of a crude log cabinet? Does not such an article abuse the idolizing powers of the pedestal?

This is the situation that confronts us in the infant of the series, the opaquely titled *Black Gold* (1989). The initial impression of immaturity has little to do with size; the piece is, in fact, perhaps the largest of the pedestals, both in height and girth. Rather, the character and the charm of the piece have to do with its resemblance to something a child might build, and with the childlike concerns it so clearly expresses and monumentalizes.

The whole arrangement has a giddy, piled-up quality, like any product of a child's irrepressible desire to add just one more block. In the haste of the moment, precise alignment and serial order cease to be concerns. The only thing that matters is that the creation stand. There are nods in this piece to the recognized order of things, but only those nods that a child would bother to give.

In the child's approach to stacking things, it is only good sense to start with something big and solid. A fat log fits the bill, particularly if that log has a conveniently flat surface. For rapidly achieving height, it is

Demilune Table
1981

expedient to use a longish wooden octagon, sprouting at an angle from the log base and tapering upward. Now we are faced with a fresh surface that begs to be occupied. A bowl looks right, familiar somehow; but it won't stay put. An adjustment to the vertical element might help, but that task would try our patience. The bowl, in the meantime, has begun to look far too ordinary. Both problems can be handily solved by putting a second, upright log on top of the whole heap. This second log mysteriously assumes the bearing of a monument, of some sort of personal treasure. It is appropriately exclamatory. It seems to merit more than just a pedestal; it deserves to sit on what sits on a pedestal.

Unlike the superseded bowl, whose elevation from kitchen table to art object is forced on us (the "bowl" is not even hollow), our memorialized log seems to be a practicing cabinet. It sports a small, comically round knob. There is no door cut into the log; instead, the log splits into two almost equal portions. The bottom of one chamber is fitted with a circular disk cut to be flush with the other side when the two sections are brought together. Apart from this platform there are no interior shelves or partitions; but then there is no true (that is, truly functional) interior, either. In fact, the log turns out to be hiding a miniature stage. A stage, of course, is for display.

This reveals something unexpected about the ultimate aspirations of *Black Gold*. By virtue of the sheer bulk of the log and its absurd posture atop the monumental bowl, by the incongruity of an apparent storage unit where an heroic figure might otherwise be, this work seems, at first, to mock all pedestal conventions. But its final word is not at all what we thought: the piece hopes to be a pedestal after all.

Cavalcade (1989) plays some tricks of its own, only one of which remotely resembles *Black Gold's*— and that in reverse. Like the latter, *Cavalcade* features an

attenuated, octagonal solid (here in ebonized mahogany) rising at an angle from a sectioned, log-like base. In contrast to the guilelessness of the child's pile, the mood of this piece is self-conscious, even studied. It flauntingly reproduces the classic gesture of the pedestal, holding aloft a simple, eminently functional platform, as if service were its sole and honorable duty.

The platform is classical in design. A solid, inverted cone of bleached lacewood tapers gently down towards two concentric necks; these rings embrace what seems to be the top of a perpendicular column disappearing into the body of the vertical support. Poised near the edge of this surface is a small, highly polished black ball. The arrangement seems to take itself altogether too seriously. The ramrod straight column, the globe in suspension on the rim of an uplifted cone: the scene is sober as a still life. That gravity, however, is quite literally and rudely interrupted by the bulk and posture of the mahogany solid below. It, too, strives valiantly to enter the Euclidean fantasy enacted overhead, but with all the grace of Bozo the Clown entering the stage on Hamlet's cue.

This piece of lumber foils all the pretensions of the somber exercise it has raised high. It offers everything, indeed, that an actual cavalcade could call for—but it offers it in all the wrong amounts. The form is crisply octagonal, but in proportions that are ludicrously huge beneath the trim cone and slender stem of the column. Though undeniably black, it does not achieve the deep, mysterious gloss of the inky ball. Most damaging of all, the element leans to one side, giving the impression that the platform is oppositely inclined, when in fact it is perfectly level. The ball thus seems to be in danger of rolling off the surface, a possibility that utterly destroys the serenity of the pose.

Cavalcade makes a lavish joke at the expense of those parts of its body it finds intolerably

sincere. The piece also offers a variation on *Black Gold's* surprise: the black ball turns out to be hollow. A hairline seam around the middle is the only indication that this object is, in fact, a container. Function has once again been put on a pedestal. With surpassingly agile wit, these pieces defy convention in every way but one: they make unlikely idols out of usefulness itself.

The title of a work often links it too closely to a single aspect of a complex identity. As a rule, Castle endows his pieces with harmless, if unenlightening, glosses on their meanings. The title of *Reality is Illusion* (1989), however, almost says too much. The phrase could be applied to anything in Castle's oeuvre.

In the present case the statement proves to have a special aptness. Of all the pieces in the pedestal group, this one is illusionistic in the most peculiar, and possibly most profound, way. While Castle's other works do funny things with function—both their own as pedestals and that of the tables, cabinets and furnishings they are ambivalently allied with—*Reality is Illusion* takes that ambivalence into another dimension. If the others are sculptures toying with the idea of becoming furniture, this object, in contrast, seems to be furniture toying with the idea of becoming sculpture. Its "reality" is maddeningly up for grabs.

The familiar, formal elements of the piece—the squat, cut-away base, with its tapering, vertical implant—appear here almost in disguise. They have been transformed into decorative objects; they speak the language of the salon, or perhaps even of the masked ball. The base wears an extraordinary coat of pressed bronze petals that climb upward in layers from the floor. The central, octagonal form is cloaked in a dark walnut veneer. Atop this element is perched an inverted hat of a bleached-mahogany platform, the rim of which spreads flamboyantly out to a

diameter almost the width of the base. A gilt ring gleams where the platform joins its bulbous posterior; and on the platform's surface waves a jaunty bronze cone, as blue-green as the base, and as feather-like.

Reality is Illusion is coy about its substance, but the truth it hides is a very strange one. We initially approach the piece as a pedestal-like object that we may or may not be inclined to use as a platform—alternatively "using" it, perhaps, as an object of contemplation. Here is where the trick has been played. For the materials of this piece, more so than those of any other members of the series, are unmistakably those of furniture. The base looks upholstered; the walnut support is veneered like a sofa leg; and the gold and ivory dish evokes nothing less than the gilded opulence of a Louis XV salon. Is the piece really furniture in masquerade?

The material illusions of *Past Joys* (1990) are equally vivid. The reality this piece conjures up is an impossible, or perhaps only an interior, one: that of memories and of dreams. Certain transformations show the hand of the mystic or the magician. Not only do particular materials seem to exhibit properties they do not, by nature, possess, but the piece as a whole represents an impossible balancing act. The precariousness of piled-up solids is made doubly fantastic by the fluidity and mobility the structure mysteriously exhibits. These qualities are concentrated in the two segmented cones that constitute both the pedestal's vertical member and its vessel, seemingly on display.

The cones have an extraordinary elemental presence; their fractures are like frozen moments in a whirlwind's spin. Between these two forces, the bowl-shaped platform seems fatefully and improbably suspended, like some freak rearrangement enacted by a dust-bowl storm. (Castle, by the way, was born in Kansas.) The whole configuration teeters on the half-moon section of an upright

The Music of Rubber Bands
1986

log. No longer the squat chunk that grounds the other works, this log stands at a dangerous angle and points upward, like a finger to the wind.

Here, perhaps more than anywhere else in the series, the functional distinctions between the parts of a pedestal are vigorously denied. The obvious, superficial resemblance of the two cones diminishes the strength of the superior position. The difference in scale seems to reflect not a material reduction of size, but the dwindling and foreshortening of receding images; the repetition hints at an infinite series.

The disposition of the cones suggests continuity of an even more startling kind: the unbroken flow of liquids from one vessel to another. With the bowl lending its bath-like presence to this illusion, the pedestal becomes a ritual font. A process of purification is indeed taking place: the weathered, patined-bronze exterior of the cones gives way, when breached, to a core of gold—as does the hard, black surface of the log. Only the bowl, in its surreal fashion, lacks an interior. Yet molten material seems to course straight through the structure, from the funnel open to the sky, to the brimming log below. *Past Joys* makes a show of penetrating to the heart of materials, but the essence thus exposed is impossibly pure—as untouchable as a dream, or indeed, as the past.

A Choir of Angels

In spite of the abundance of carved seating Castle made at the beginning of his career, his work has generally reflected great ambivalence about the chair. Its properties seem never to have been one of his abiding concerns. *Stool Sculpture,* for example, represents a perch for a bird or an animal almost more than it does a prop (or a crutch) for a human being. *Scribe Stool* is primarily a sculptural study in hierarchies of scale, balance, and vertical order. The dramatic and successful reappearance of the chair in the current series thus invites a reassessment of the form as it has erratically appeared in the course of the artist's career.

The chairs, settees, and other seating arrangements Castle made in the 1960s evolved out of the essentially sculptural approach with which he began. His early stack-laminated works are monolithic. They seldom seem composed of separate parts, no matter how many functionally distinct areas they may comprise. The lamination process itself, as Castle employed it, embodies a monolithic principle: it yields a hunk of wood of sufficient size and shape to be carved down to a single form. The character of the furniture made in this way is unmistakably organic. Its plain surfaces, untouched by paint or veneer, have all the continuity and coherence of a plant or other living thing. Every feature seems virtually continous with the rest of the body, sharing, as it were, its lifeblood.

Some of the carved chairs look like blossoms opening over thick stems; others, supported by a spread of muscular tentacles, suggest the concavity of a mollusk. Particular functional components—back, arms, and legs—are seldom unambiguously visible as such. The impression of the continuous, irregular curvature of a living body is at least as dominant.

On such a body, any flat plane or angularity looks unnatural. The table surfaces, for example, of Castle's organic works have an invasive character. *Wall Table's* functional surface appears as no more than a horizontal slice off the top of a bent, tubal form; similarly, all the planar surfaces in the early carved furniture come across as ruthless interruptions of the organic whole.

Given these inherent limitations, it is not surprising that Castle eventually abandoned the organic style to explore traditional joinery. Immediately thereafter, chairs ceased to play the leading role in his repertoire. Castle continued to make chairs throughout the 1970s and 1980s; but much of this furniture—such as the *Crescent*

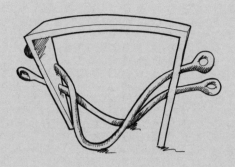

Rocker (1972) and the popular *Alpha* and *Zephyr* chairs (1974)—incorporates highly standardized features, including four-point support, clearly articulated arms and legs, and upholstery. Whatever sculptural interest these pieces have, they lack the subversive energy and intensity that Castle lavished on many of his tables. That genius is reincarnated in his Angel Chairs.

The Angel Chairs flow directly from themes introduced and elaborated by Castle's warped-top tables. A major achievement of the warped-tops was a new flexibility—so graphically symbolized by the bowed tops—for the table surface. It has neither to be flat nor in any other way to suffer the tabletop's traditional, servile lot. The Pedestal Pieces enthusiastically exploit this freedom by reducing the surface area of the ostensible top and claiming for it interests independent of the function of support.

The Angel Chairs are alive with these discoveries. The principle they embody to greatest effect is one they share most obviously with *The Music of Rubber Bands*: the juxtaposition, and even interpenetration, of starkly opposed elements. *The Music of Rubber Bands* is a study in such radical contrasts. Black, bending, tubal forms are interlocked with pale, hard, angular ones. More than just these contrasts, though, the nature of the conjunction is what matters. Geometric, planar features appear as separate and independent forms; they exist alongside, rather than being ruthlessly carved out of, irregular or organic ones. The radical opposition of distinct elements within a single work represents an extraordinary departure from Castle's monochromatic and monolithic works of the 1960s. His current series of chairs develops these relationships in a way that neither the uniformly organic, laminated works nor the single-minded furniture that followed ever could.

Castle's return to freer methods of sculpting the stack-lamination—he now often carves with a chainsaw—has generated familiar organic shapes. The central, winged form of the chairs retains the powerful bodily coherence that was both the outstanding feature and the ultimate liability of the earlier stack-laminated works. In the Angel Chairs, that integrity becomes an asset. The sense of wholeness is partly due to the obvious and powerful figural connotations the chairs have. They are informed not only by the idea of the wing chair, but also by the idea of the wing itself.

Instruments of airborne mobility, wings are natural emblems of the will to overcome the earth-bound requirement of support. It is no wonder that the form has such fascination for Castle, who has turned to it on a number of occasions in the course of his career. One such instance, a desk called *Victory* (1980), contains the most dramatic representation of the wing before its appearance as such a dominant feature of the Angel Chairs. The desk is the last of the naturally finished, stack-laminated furniture that Castle carved before abandoning the style altogether. Like *Ghost Clock*, this piece offers some compelling insights into the very genre to which it bids adieu.

In certain respects, *Victory* is typical of its kind. It is dominated by a massive, sculpted base, to which Castle added a table surface supposedly as an afterthought. Afterthought or not, the presence of the top in *Victory* is significant. It does not amount to the crass exposure, by horizontal slicing, of the interior of a body, but instead comes across as one of its natural features. *Victory* has not, like so many others, been fragmented into base and tabletop. The wing form, which suggests soaring mobility instead of recumbent support, establishes the flat surface as an integral part—not a disruptive modification—of an organic form. Function is here a natural, if incidental, property of the sculpted object, which makes no material sacrifice on function's behalf. *Victory* approaches a sculptural freedom of the kind achieved by the Angel Chairs; in both

Victory
1980

cases, the wing is the instrument and proud symbol of that accomplishment.

Angel of Blind Justice (1990), the darkest presence in Castle's strange choir, is as ruthless as its name suggests. This ebonized-mahogany figure seems to be perched on the edge of some rocky overhang, or to rule from the peak of a mountain. Its very blackness gives it the abstraction of a three-dimensional silhouette, of something seen from a great distance. The wings' exterior, uniformly pocked with cuts flowing roughly in the same direction, has the solid, sculpted look of a Renaissance angel's feathers. This creature could as easily be Lucifer's emissary—a bat out of hell—as any raging Gabriel of God.

There lurks, indeed, something of the warrior. The concave maple slab that penetrates the winged body resembles a shield. Its presence constitutes an act of violence perpetrated on the wings, which seem to convulse around the intruder without otherwise faltering. The arcing surface of the slab suggests an object under tension, its shape bowed by the sheer force of the black body that embraces it. This element's ostensible function as a seat seems strictly incidental. No idealization of the chair, which makes a seat its center and arms and legs its servants, permeates the structure of this piece. The slab of a seat is cantilevered out on both sides, supported only where it meets and passes through the wings, extending an equal distance either way.

If we understand the piece as support and enclosure for the human body, the wings appear to offer a frontal embrace. The mythic spectacle the figure first evokes, however, is an inescapable vision in the end. On that windy precipice, Blind Justice assumes the crouch of a raptor, uplifted wings spread out behind. This sightless bird of prey accepts no riders, making its formidable descent and unerring judgments alone.

Harmonious Opportunities (1990) presents an image far more serene. An attitude of embrace is the dominant impression here. The wings, cocked at a less exclamatory angle, extend forward in a gentle, inward curve. Their ebonized-mahogany surfaces are more coarsely cut and carved, and incised with streaks of blue and green. The colors bring both wind and sea into the repertoire of elemental powers seemingly at the disposal of this creature. It, like Blind Justice, is not entirely of the earth. The spirit, however, is a benevolent one.

The difference in temper is accomplished partly by the seat. Its shimmering, avodire veneer exudes a warmth entirely foreign to the cooly understated surface of Blind Justice's sloping shield. There, the element enters the body of the wings at an angle, accentuating the aggressive, reared-up posture of the piece. In Harmonious Opportunities, the oblong slab lies perfectly flat and runs parallel to the ground. It passes cleanly through the black concavity, with none of the tension of its bowed counterpart in Blind Justice.

The seat function once again has an arbitrary quality. This time, however, the generous expanse of Harmonious Opportunities welcomes occupancy. Its two big wings invite, rather than threaten, a pair of sitters. Unlike Blind Justice, which is deeply self-absorbed, the piece is animated throughout by the spirit of cooperation. Hardly the clamorous herald of our fates confronting us in Blind Justice, Harmonious Opportunities has an earthly calling. Embodying the very virtue that gave the seat its name, it is sedate.

Bolstered Egos (1990) and Supported Affections (1990) add to the wings and the seat a third element of equal simplicity, the bronze cone. In Castle's vocabulary, the cone is an emblem of ambivalent support. The performance of the cones in Bolstered Egos is particularly

dubious. They tilt inward on their edges, lifting the corners of an amorphous mahogany drape that sags convincingly between pinpoint supports. The stark, black shape seems almost to liquify as it flows through a four-sided, sloping curve of a back and out the other side, ending in a limp trail on the floor. The rich grain of an avodire veneer is just as fluid, washing up from the sides of the back towards its center.

Like some of the imagery in Castle's Pedestal Pieces, this scene approaches an almost classical austerity. The self-conscious arrangement has the deliberate disposition of a still life. Like the still lifes enacted by the pedestals, however, this one defeats the very principle it represents. The tips of cones are hardly adequate props for their unwieldy, weighty burden—much less for the human frame. Even unoccupied, the dark pocket of the seat threatens to pull its conical moorings to the floor.

Bolstered Egos sets up relationships only to insure their inevitable collapse. The cones will fall, the drape will drop, the slender back will complete its trajectory towards the floor. Just about the only pairing that seems likely to survive is that of the black drape and the slab it penetrates. These two egos are bolstered indeed, but not in the way we expect; they depend not on the cones, but on each other, for support.

Supported Affections (1990) is even more elusive. A great, startling drape of ebonized mahogany droops once more between two upright cones, backed this time by the smooth, curly-maple veneer of a curved polygon. This concave slab rests at an angle, thus gaining some stability of its own. Again, the themes are vaguely classical, and the message turns out to be just as mixed. The posture of the cones at first seems correct; but then one of them lifts a surly lip just slightly off the floor. The hammocky swath of seat seems in danger of certain impalement by the unscrupulous cones. Like the cones, the seat makes a discreet but all-important gesture of autonomy: it arches up improbably on one side, sustaining an angle in midair with no support at all. The black ribbon of a seat continues stiffly, merely grazing rather than falling around the tip of the right-hand cone. The cone appears to have drifted from its proper place, carelessly exposing its pretense of support. The whole tableau turns out to be a sham. As with *Bolstered Egos*, the truth of the work resides in a peculiar relationship between two contrasting parts. They are barely, but genuinely, interlocked.

In that tentative union lies a metaphor for our own participation in these works. Ever insisting on their independence from our needs, refusing to be reduced to whatever we might use them for, these pieces still extend a sly invitation to the furniture dance. However self-involved the pedestals and chairs may seem, one watchful and seductive eye is ever trained on us, appealing to our wish to sit, to store, to place on top of—in short, to make ourselves at home.

Home is where these works began and it is where they end. To be sure, the pedestals have summoned up a universe divine, a hidden realm we idolize but up to which—Saint Simeon notwithstanding—we can never climb. The Angel Chairs have opened like apocalyptic maws, their wings a flapping welcome to the fiery pit or else the sails by which to rise, in the homeliest of postures, to our ultimate reward.

Those are their stories. Wendell Castle's pieces, like all masters of the fabulist's art, know how to make their listeners heroes of the tales they tell. His objects welcome us in the way that only furniture can, but give us much more than furniture ever could. That, in the end, is our true and very bright reward.

Furniture, Philosophy, Craft, and Art:
The Masterwork of Wendell Castle

Arthur C. Danto

*Arthur C. Danto is Johnsonian Professor of Philosophy at Columbia University. He has been art critic for **The Nation** magazine since 1984 and is the author of, most recently, **Encounters and Reflections: Art in the Historical Present** (Farrar, Straus, Giroux 1990).*

It has been the settled ambition of the studio-furniture movement, and most particularly of Wendell Castle as its acknowledged leader, to traverse what has seemed to be an arbitrary boundary dividing fine furniture from the fine arts, and to get the movement's masterwork accepted in the higher category. It is something of an irony that in the very first discussions of the metaphysics of art, in Plato's *Republic,* the ambition would have been precisely the reverse: to overcome the distance between works of art and products of craftsmanship so that art might attain that higher degree of reality ascribed by Plato to such things as beds.

In the famous scheme, there were three orders of reality to consider: that of the Forms (or Ideas); that of objects embodying these Forms; and, finally and lowest, that of works of art, which at their best but imitate these things. Plato's examples were the Form of the Bed; the actual beds craftsmen make and in which we get born, sleep, make love, and die; and finally, the mere imitations of beds, as these might be found on the sides of Greek vases or cups.

Plato had little doubt as to the metaphysical inferiority of the imitation of beds in art. It was part of his overall endeavor to discredit art as of little philosophical, and even less human, significance in the ideal republic. Part of his dismissal rested on a claim that the craftsman possesses knowledge, while the artist does not. Indeed, throughout the great dialogues in which Socrates advances Plato's philosophical agenda, it is the carpenter, the craftsman, the smith, the person who possesses knowledge of how to do things, who is the personification of the kind of knowledge to which we should all aspire.

A second basis for Plato's mistrust of art was that it trafficked in mere appearances, which it endeavored to get its viewers to believe were real. The artist not only lacks knowledge of reality, according to Plato's indictment, but is duplicitous enough to congratulate himself on his ability to provoke false beliefs. That art has been able to meet and overcome this complex indictment, and to achieve a degree of acceptance, and even prestige, such that furniture-makers now aspire to have their products considered as at least art's equal, is one of the great, triumphant reversals in the history of thought. Plato would clearly have considered the furniture-makers' ambition unintelligible.

Few today subscribe, without heavy qualification, to Plato's metaphysics of art. What metaphysics of art is it, then, that we *do* subscribe to that could make sense of the furniture-makers' ambition? It is difficult to answer the question without defining art, a pretty daunting business. The nebulousness of art's definition has thwarted the furniture-makers, and kept them in the place they have lately sought to escape.

One shortcut to the realm of art suggested itself early on in the studio-furniture movement. Whatever the definition of art might be, sculpture would have been widely accepted as a fine art. Because furniture and sculpture have in common three-dimensionality and movability, perhaps the way to get furniture accepted as art is by first getting it accepted as sculpture! If we could demonstrate how arbitrary the line is between furniture and sculpture, then furniture would have as clear a claim to arthood as sculpture has.

Two strategies have recommended themselves. One has been that of Scott Burton, whose tactic was to insist that at least *his* furniture was sculpture, and then to browbeat critics and collectors into either accepting this proclamation, or giving good reasons for saying that his tables and chairs were not sculpture. Since no one really has a much clearer definition of sculpture than of art, Burton almost succeeded in getting his things acknowledged as sculpture. All he really did, though, was

make his critics feel uncomfortable. Burton's pieces still looked like and were generally treated as furniture. They may be *art,* and the artworld was prepared to allow as much, but not sculpture. There had to be a more direct way to become art than by attempting to pass as sculpture.

The same might be said of the second strategy, which was to disguise the fact that something was furniture by getting it to look like a piece of sculpture. That is what Wendell Castle endeavored to achieve through his famous *Stool Sculpture,* as it was retroactively titled, of 1959. The strategy was to enter it in a juried sculpture show as a piece of sculpture, get the jury to accept the work as such— and then, upon revealing that it was really a stool and hence an article of furniture, to get the members of the jury to admit that they could not really tell the difference. The point could not have been more classically philosophical: if you cannot *tell* the difference, there really *is* no difference. The difference is merely empirical, when it exists at all, and not principled. Unfortunately, that does not make furniture into sculpture; it just erases the borderline between them by causing false beliefs. This is what Plato faulted artists for doing long ago; Castle showed himself to be an artist in Plato's sense.

Castle was able to achieve this feat in part because sculpture no longer had any prescribed form. One could not have done the same thing in 1890, for example, when sculpture was still figural, and largely realistic and allegorical. It would have been inordinately difficult to fashion a stool that could not have been told apart from, say, *The Kiss* by Rodin. By 1960, however, abstract sculpture was an available option, and Castle's work looks very much like a straightforward wood sculpture of the era. Indeed, it is possible to imagine a piece, outwardly like *Stool Sculpture* in every respect, which was simply intended as a sculpture. That it could be sat in would have been an irrelevancy or an oversight. Castle had only to mask the piece's function, by making his stool look as little like a prototypical stool as possible. To sit on my imagined piece of sculpture would be a misuse or an abuse of it. One would hesitate to impose one's bodily weight on its fragile-looking structure. But Castle had *designed* his piece to be sat on, assuming one knew where to place one's body. Draped among its crutch-like forms, the human body might resemble something one could have seen in a Surrealist painting of a few years before. The sculpture that the stool outwardly resembles might itself come from Surrealism. The piece has the look of Moore, or of Noguchi.

Whatever the influences, and however handsome the object, there was clearly in the end something wrong with the strategy. One saw the piece as sculpture only if one did not know it to be furniture. The illusion dissolved once one knew it to be a stool, albeit an eccentric one. The original disjunction between furniture and sculpture remained. If one aspires to the status of art, disguise as a method is finally as unavailing as the angry classificatory fiats issued by Scott Burton. Clearly a better strategy has to be discovered.

Stool Sculpture is nevertheless testimony to the singular philosophical intelligence that elevates Wendell Castle above his fellow furniture artists. The very idea that the true identity of the object should reveal itself through an act of transformative perception is evidence of the philosophical character of the piece, construed as an exercise in the ambiguity of identity. In a way, *Stool Sculpture* possesses the same ineradicable ambiguity illustrated in the celebrated Duck-Rabbit illusion, which first entered

philosophical discourse through Ludwig Wittgenstein's *Philosophical Investigations*. Looked at one way, the drawing depicts a rabbit; looked at another way, a duck. What we are unable to see is the rabbit and the duck at the same time. Wittgenstein observes that if the picture had been shown to him, "I might never have seen anything but a rabbit in it."

Had Castle not disclosed *Stool Sculpture*'s other identity, it might have passed into history as a fairly ordinary, advanced wooden sculpture of the late 1960s, unmistakably of its art-historical moment, rather than what it is: a meditation in the medium of wood on an ambiguity between sculpture and furniture. Whatever Castle supposed *Stool Sculpture* demonstrated, one lesson clearly emerges from its philosophical complexity as a work. If furniture is to be art, it must be art *as* furniture. It must be at once art *and* furniture.

Castle's pieces often conceal their identity as furniture in such a way that it comes as a surprise that they do, after all, have a use as a cabinet, say, or a chest. There is a quality of surprise and pleasure in first encountering these latent functions, as when a hidden door opens to reveal a set of shelves or a storage space or a niche. A piece will still look handsome and often abstract enough to be taken as a piece of sculpture, but then its truth as a piece of furniture is abruptly revealed. The ingenuity and wit with which one discovers this truth fortify our appreciation of so many of Castle's works, and are among their cognitive hallmarks.

Consider, for example, a work with an awesomely Platonistic title, *Into Reality,* of 1989. It is composed of three elements, each of which has the look of a blunt and lopped-off log, elegantly spiraled in such a way that the pattern argues with the keg-like forms. One "log" is horizontal, and another, vertical, balances the third, which stands poised on its point, like a tubby ballerina. The lower horizontal element has a function, one might say, but not a use. In Castle's words, it "ends up as a balance for the whole thing." That is, its function is defined with reference to the other components of the piece, and so is internal to it, whereas "use" is external and implies a user. "The two that stand up vertically are hollow in order to create a cabinet," Castle comments, adding, "it is disguised utility." The remark evinces a deep attitude that virtually defines this artist's outlook. In every instance, the truth that is revealed behind the disguise is the piece's identity as furniture. The basic question remains unresolved. Given its truth as furniture, what makes it art when it is art?

Let us approach this question by paying some attention to what it is in which the truth of furniture consists; to what it is, in other words, that cannot be subtracted from furniture, though it clearly can be, and has been, subtracted from art. I refer to the vexed notion of *use*—to the idea that something is intended to be sat in or written on or filled with things that it preserves and protects. Somehow the idea of use has come to be a stigma to furniture artists, as though it were cause for embarrassment. Ever since the writing of Kant, not having a use has been an aesthetic ideal. It appeared intermittently in the nineteenth century and has become epidemic in our own.

Some deep and untraversable disjunction seems to exist between works of art and articles of use; it becomes impossible for something to be both a piece of furniture (from which use *cannot* be subtracted) and a work of art. It would be interesting to know how this dandified vision of art should have so penetrated our consciousness that the paradigm of artistic excellence should be the person who does nothing, who has no use, who simply exists. There are, of course, Eastern traditions, such as that of the Tao, in which doing nothing has been elevated to a way of being; but in the Western tradition, as elsewhere in

the East, utility can be defended as the very basis of our moral being and the source of all values. It was so defended, for example, by David Hume in his great *Enquiry Concerning the Principles of Morals:*

In common life, we may observe, that the circumstance of utility is always appealed to; nor is it supposed, that a greater eulogy can be given to any man, than to display usefulness to the public, and enumerate the services, which he has performed to mankind and society. What praise, even of an inanimate form, if the regularity and elegance of its parts destroy not its fitness for any useful purpose! And how satisfactory an apology for any disproportion or seeming deformity, if we can show the necessity of that particular construction for the use intended! A ship appears more beautiful to an artist, or one moderately skilled in navigation, where its prow is wide and swelling beyond its poop, than if it were framed with a precise geometrical regularity, in contradiction to all the laws of mechanics. A building, whose doors and windows were exact squares, would hurt the eye by that very proportion; as ill adapted to the figure of a human creature, for whose service the fabric was intended.

Hume's utilitarianism implies a familiar aesthetic: form should be defined by function. The beauty of the ship is that ages of making ships has given every element the shape efficient use requires. Castle's aesthetic is almost the exactly the reverse of this, partly in consequence of his philosophy of disguise and discovery. Asked to identify a precedent for this counter-functional aesthetic, I would probably name Michelangelo, especially as an architect. At the entranceway to the Laurentian Library in Florence, for example, Michelangelo places gigantesque volutes on either side of the door. A volute usually serves as a supportive bracket of some high, horizontal element, such as a cornice, which the volutes hold up. The size of Michelangelo's volutes implies a very heavy burden, a suggestion contradicted by the relative lightness of the door frame. (The frame is, in any case, vertical rather than horizontal, and needs no support.) The artist has laid the volutes on their backs, contradicting their customary placement. This brilliantly witty and allusive play with architectural elements defines the spirit of mannerist ornamentation, which is precisely the spirit of Castle's work throughout its mature phase.

Hume would never have thought the absence of a use was a commendatory, let alone a defining, trait of works of art. He appreciated works of art as having important uses, which art has been felt to possess in every age and culture except our own. In recent decades it has been the practice to appreciate art in terms of formalistic analysis, and to regard everything that does not contribute to formal structure as a kind of irrelevancy or excrescence.

The distinction between the practical and the aesthetic was formulated by Kant. Art was to exist primarily, if not exclusively, for the sake of distinterested contemplation. It was to be a source of aesthetic pleasure uncontaminated by the squalor of practicality. Kant's formulations did not become mainstream aesthetics until revived by Clement Greenberg, who considered Kant's *Critique of Aesthetic Judgment* the greatest work ever composed on the philosophy of art. Greenberg's immense prestige in New York art circles made this teaching the official stance, widely adopted by art critics and by curators. When certain art museums, such as the Museum of Modern Art in New York City, actually showed objects of utility, it was because these were viewed as exemplars of good design, rather than as works of art.

The concept of use thus became a stigma for furniture-makers concerned to be artists. It was something to be ashamed of, something to be concealed, something to be subverted. One of the most remarkable things about Wendell Castle is the creativity he was able to

marshal in disguising and subverting utility. At times one is convinced that utility is for him a burden, something he would joyfully jettison to become a sculptor, free of utility's imperatives. In fact, use is essential to the art he practices. Use is logically implied by the concept of furniture and cannot be eliminated. Use is not essential to art, but that hardly means that furniture cannot be art. It means, rather, that when furniture is art, its use is essential to its status as such.

Once use is categorically accepted, certain things follow. Viewing is a very narrow relationship to be confined to, though it seems to have been decided that this is the only relationship relevant to the enjoyment of art. It reduces us in our experience of art to our eyes, as if the rest of our body were there only as the bearer of the optical system, moving the eyes nearer and farther away, or carrying them around a statue. Our hands, our feet, our behinds, and our sexes are dematerialized in the aesthetic process. Should someone get physically excited, say, by the painting of a nude, aestheticians and art historians would hasten to point out that this was a wrong response.

A lot of our bodily movements are certainly relevant to our appreciation of furniture. Furniture refers to us as essentially embodied; as agents, rather than visual patients; as beings who stand and sit, lean and lie, recline and repose, who open and close, place and re-place, work and play, and who deploy our bodies in innumerable ways. Between us and a chair there is none of that deadening and insulating aesthetic distance that reduces us to parts of what we are, and across which we can merely gaze, as over an aesthetic no-man's-land. Furniture addresses us in our essential humanity. It may be argued that this is true whether the furniture is art or not; but we might observe, in response, that neither is every picture a work of pictorial art.

One criterion by which furniture might be measured as art has suggested itself, strongly at times, to Wendell Castle. It is the criterion of superb craftsmanship, which returns us to Plato's bed-builder. Whatever Castle touches exemplifies craftsmanship in the highest degree. In fact, he at one point supposed that if the craft were supreme, it must *ipso facto* turn into art, as if nothing further were needed. Craft would turn the caterpillar of utility into the butterfly of fine art.

According to the critic Joseph Giovannini, Castle felt in 1981 that "he had assembled in his studio what was perhaps the best group of woodworkers ever to work under the same roof, but . . . he felt 'stuck'." He felt stuck, evidently, because his work was not receiving the high prices works of art were beginning to command. For Castle, it was simple inference that his work must not have been accepted as art. Castle's dealer, Alexander Milliken, then encouraged him to "make a piece of furniture that would arguably be the best piece ever made." The implication was that further craftsmanly effort would carry the piece across the line. Indeed, a number of critics later recognized, in Giovannini's phrase, the "artistic potential of Castle's craft." Artistic *potential*! All that fine and fancy handwork—the shaping, sanding, joining, polishing, inlaying, lacquering, gold-leafing—and still only *artistic potential*? *Was the work not smooth enough? Not adequately joined?* John Russell had the sense that "something difficult has been done to perfection." Since perfection is what you cannot do better than, it is plain that no extension of craftsmanship is going to effect the transformation. If the work is ever going to be art, it must already be art, and has to have been art before the effort inspired by Milliken ever began. The higher prices were consolation, but the philosophical progress remained obscure.

The masterpiece that Castle produced on this occasion was the breathtakingly exquisite *Lady's Desk with Two Chairs* of 1981, in the collection of Peter T. Joseph. Years later Castle observed, "It was a point in my thinking when I thought exquisite workmanship would become art." As if craftsmanship were the tunnel and art the light at the end of it! "That turned out to be a difficult concept," he added laconically. It may have occurred to him by then that a fair amount of the advanced sculpture of the time was incontestably art (at least so the experts maintained), but by no stretch of the imagination did it display or require craft.

The Detroit Institute of Arts, which showed a remarkable forwardness of thought in mounting the stunning exhibition of Castle's work in 1989, manifested a similar adventurousness in putting on the first posthumous exhibition of the work of Eva Hesse in 1972. Hesse used as her materials such things as rope, cheesecloth, balloons, Plexiglas and latex. The material was industrial, commonplace, and ugly, and in many cases the work was subject to almost instant deterioration. Hesse's work was defiantly anti-aesthetic. In an interview published in the month of her death in 1970, she responded to the term "decorative" with a violent antipathy, as if the concept ran contrary to everything in which she believed as an artist.

Castle and his artisans were turning out works one might describe as *defiantly* decorative and crafted to their last inch, making use of birdseye maple, purpleheart, satinwood, lacewood, mahogany, walnut, and gold leaf. Sculptors of the cutting edge, in the meantime, were working under the same ideology as Hesse, employing industrial plywood, chicken wire, broken glass, vinyl, string, cinder blocks, and molten lead—and endorsing a kind of brutality of look. They used the most most primitive possible processes, leaning slabs of wood or rusted steel against a wall, strewing shattered glass randomly on the floor. These sculptors were accepted as artists. They were written up glowingly in *Artforum* and *October,* and their works fetched prices equal to Castle's and perhaps today well in excess of them. A skein of latex-soaked rope by Eva Hesse will bring a price at auction, even in today's depressed market, that makes Castle's work a steal. Small wonder that craft came to seem to Castle "a difficult concept!"

In the Arts and Crafts movement of the nineteenth century, one would have been hard pressed to distinguish art from craft. It was an unquestioned assumption that art already involved craft to a great degree. What was required was to bring furniture to the point where it had as much craft in it as painting and sculpture were assumed to have. One had to reintroduce into furniture-making the handcraft that it had lost to industrial manufacturing.

Art-making, in contrast, had never been industrialized. It was the paradigm of a preindustrial activity in the age of industrialization, and served as the movement's model for making furniture and decorative objects generally. To make fine furniture as it had been made a century before was like rediscovering a lost art.

Drawing and painting, like carving and molding, required extreme skill in order to achieve resemblances that would meet the prevailing conventions, and to create the sorts of illusions on which the understanding of those arts depended. It would never have occurred to the thinkers of the Arts and Crafts movement that there would come a time when the "arts" were not "crafts." The experience of the 1970s and the 1980s, however, demonstrates that something can be art, even very important art, without having craft, and certainly without having much by way of beauty.

Crafted furniture is labor-intensive to an extreme degree, but being cunningly handmade is not what makes it art. It is far from plain that a manufactured chair cannot be a work of art. The concept of art might include something manufactured, but exclude something made by skilled hands. On the other hand, when a piece of furniture in which intense craft has been invested turns out to be a work of art as well, then part of its identity as a work of art may come from the manifest skills that entered into its making. With Castle's works this is certainly true. They proclaim their craft and, up to a point, that proclamation figures into their identity as art. But only, I think, up to a point—a point at which a fair amount of what one might call "furniture criticism" stops. The furniture critic is literate in the language of craft; he or she can speak knowingly about grains and joints, identify rare woods and point to precedents. We have to go beyond that, however, before we begin to broach the dominion of art. We have to enter the realm of meaning.

Let us consider a well-known, cast-iron sculpture of a chair, done in 1973 by Joel Shapiro. What is especially striking about Shapiro's chair is its scale: it is about three inches high. It cannot be sat in by anything larger than a small doll. It is clear, however, that Shapiro did not shrink the chair to miniature dimensions in order to subvert function. He did this in part to give intensity to the space the chair was intended to dominate. To make its power felt, that very small "chair" requires a very large room. The piece belongs on the floor, like a "real" chair, and it ought to be the only object in the room.

The ordinariness of Shapiro's chair connects it with its place in the history of sculpture: the piece marks a break with the abstract tradition in which Shapiro had participated and is energized by its repudiation of that tradition. The chair belongs to an art history. One of the problems facing Castle is precisely his lack of an historical location. To be more exact, he has the wrong kind of historical location in the minds of the art critics, who see him in terms of the traditions of the *ébéniste* and hence the tradition of craft.

In truth, Castle is undertaking something monumental and heroic. He is taking on the art history of his time by insisting that furniture as furniture can have a place in it. His work rejects a history in which being art excludes having a function, just as Shapiro's chair rejected a history that excluded as art whatever had content.

Historical location plays a central role in something's identity as a work of art. Something can be a work of art at one time, when something else exactly like it would not have been a work of art at another time. We cannot tell whether something is an artwork merely by examining it, or by working with a checklist of observable properties. We have to know the complex of possibilities in the history that explains that object's being.

Shapiro's chair further depends for its artistic force on the fact that it has the content it has, that it really is "of" a chair. A chair stands in a very different relation to a room than some abstract piece of patined bronze would do. An abstraction might relate to a space, but not to a room. A chair belongs in a room; it stands, as furniture, in an internal relationship to a room because it is rooms that chairs furnish. This brings us to the concept of meaning, especially the kind of meaning possessed by articles of furniture. A set of meanings is inevitably implied by the content of Shapiro's minuscule, cast-iron effigy; for pieces of furniture, and chairs in particular, are heavily charged with meanings in virtue of the functions they perform in human life.

I have elsewhere written about the chair as a subject in art, as in Van Gogh's paintings of his chair and Gauguin's chair. These are virtually portraits of the two artists as chairs, and the selection of these particular chairs dramatizes the singular complex of meanings in which chairs are implicated. Think of chairs as elements in a silent language of furniture, where the language defines the life lived by those who use the furniture.

Fill in the picture to which Castle's astonishing ladies' desks with their two chairs refer us. Consider what it means to be a lady sitting at one of those desks, with a confidante—or a lover—seated in the other chair (or with the other chair significantly empty, and not just abstractly unoccupied) when the lady is at her desk. Those desks condense the entire institution of ladyhood! Or think of the way the salon chair facilitates life as lived out in the French salon, where the chair can be carried from conversation to conversation, or arranged for string trios, or sat on as one discourses while balancing a cream puff on a plate of fragile porcelain. Compare that chair with the English wing-chair, solid and immobile, sheltering and isolating, surrounding its occupant with silence, warmth, and palpable security. We make statements about ourselves by the chairs we use as eloquently as we do by the clothes we choose. If we are indifferent to what we sit on or wear, that too is a statement we make. There is no such thing as a semiotically innocent use. We are what we use.

Putting to one side the chairs that we find in art, and the statements artists make through chairs as subjects, we still do not know how to distinguish chairs that are art from chairs that are just chairs. We are, however, beginning to approach the border of the concept we need. Once more, it is best to approach it a bit obliquely. Let us, for purposes of comparison, consider texts. All texts are made of words, as is this text. All have meanings in terms of their uses. This is a philosophical text, intended to orient its readers in a certain conceptual terrain. The text aims to clarify. Recall all the texts one encounters in a day—newspaper articles, recipes, love letters, directions for putting a washstand together, business reports, yesterday's diary entry, overdue bills. Among these are some that are works of art, even of literary art. They may or may not be distinguished from other texts by virtue of their craft; but a newspaper article can be as crafted as a sonnet, and an overdue bill from the insurance company is a masterpiece of economy. Aristotle observes, with his usual acuity, that history does not become poetry by someone putting it into rhyme. The difference is that poetry is universal and history is particular—but nothing about the texts as texts will tell us which is which.

A start is made when one realizes that works of literature provide metaphors for their users, who will henceforward see their lives metaphorically as the life of Huckleberry Finn or Anna Karenina or Rabbit Angstrom. The same is true for furniture when it is art. It creates metaphors for its users. Art furniture can do this because articles of furniture carry meanings through their relationships to one another, to our dwellings, to our lives, and above all, to our bodies. To sit in a chair is to perform a meaningful act. One cannot sink into a salon chair. One sits in order to rise, the way a bird lights on a bough in order to take flight. One sinks into a wing chair, finding shelter from the world. It is these sorts of meanings, such as perching and being enveloped, that then begin to make possible the metaphors of furniture as art.

Let us contemplate some examples from the present exhibition. *Dark Secrets* (1990) has a subtitle: *Ladder-back Chair with Mountain*. The ladder-back chair is a very familiar form, and a favorite one in the American suburban living room because of its connotations of Early American or Colonial style. Of course, the word "ladder" in "ladder-back" is something of an extended use of the term, much in the way in which "arms" and "legs" are used in reference to a chair's anatomy. What Castle has done is to fashion an actual ladder as this chair's back. By itself, this might simply be a flight of wit, more a clever joke than a metaphor; but in fact the ladder carries two meanings.

One is that of a ladder back, and the other is that of a ladder. The "mountain" goes with one of the meanings, and the fact that the piece is a chair goes with the other. The metaphor is that of sitting beside a ladder next to a mountain, hence of being out of doors when one in fact is indoors. The piece dramatizes the space that it is to be set in, making it ambiguously indoors and outdoors.

My sense is that the metaphor in *Dark Secrets* derives from the fact that it belongs in a series of chairs, each of which makes reference to angels. Once the angelic reference is in place, one may think about the dream of Jacob in the Book of Genesis, Chapter 28. Jacob there beholds a *ladder set up on the earth, and the top of it reached to heaven; and behold, the angels of God were ascending and descending on it.* The ladder thus implies a fairly complex narrative, which brings into the experience references to earth and heaven, and Jacob having a vision on the desert floor with a silhouetted mountain in the distance. The experience requires that we interact with the piece, that we sit beneath and against the ladder. It was a powerful dream for Jacob and it is a powerful experience for the sitter, who is transformed by the chair in dramatic fashion. The chair certainly means a lot more than a highly crafted device for taking a load off your feet, and it makes possible an experience unavailable from painting and sculpture.

Let me add, in case my reading seems extravagant, that the companion piece, also using a ladder and an angelic presence, has as its title *True Dreams* (1990). One might also consider the rather mysterious clock called *Time is Man's Angel* (1990), with its Jacob's ladder of stacked drawers rising at an angle out of a mountain, and sur-mounted by an angelic black sphere with golden wings. Perhaps the angel announces when time is up, like a figure in the Revelation.

The series of Angel Chairs inevitably awakens an echo of Rainer Maria Rilke's first *Duino Elegy:*

Who, if I cried out, would hear me among the angelic orders? As he did with the literalization of the ladder(back), Castle gives us in these chairs a literalization of the wings in the winged chair, and then metaphorically transfers the wings to dark angels. Being enwrapped in angelic wings is another order of metaphor altogether:

Even if one of them suddenly
pressed me against his heart, I should fade in the strength of his
stronger existence. For Beauty's nothing
but beginning of Terror we're still just able to bear,
and why we adore it so is because it serenely
disdains to destroy us. Each single angel is terrible.

These are pretty powerful metaphorical enactments. Angels are, after all, not just downy, cuddly, flying creatures. They are, as the word's origin implies, announcers and message-bearers, coming with shattering communications from other places. Think of the Angel of the Annunciation, or the Angel of the Expulsion, or the various tidings-bringers of the Old and New Testaments.

What lightens the portent of black angels is the lightness of touch in these pieces, their cleverness, craft, and wit. The metaphor leaves intact the fact that these are chairs, even winged chairs, so that danger and security combine their ordinarily warring meanings. The experience of one who sits in them may be like that of a child being told scary things in the security of his bed.

Jacob took the stone he had used as a pillow while he was having his dream, and turned it on end to make what the Bible calls a pillar, which is really a pedestal. Jacob poured oil on top of it and declared it God's house, which brings us to the next series of pieces gathered here, Castle's Pedestal Pieces.

To put something "on a pedestal" is to acknowledge its preciousness as against other objects, and to put someone on a pedestal is to treat him or her as if that person stood above the crosscurrent of ordinary life—as one treats a work of art or a god. The pedestal literally lifts whatever is set upon it onto a higher plane than is commonly occupied by objects of use, such as dishes and tools. Pedestal height is generally too inconvenient, relative to the height of the human body, for work. Beyond that, the surface area of the pedestal is usually too restricted. Height and diameter together tend to thwart use and emphasize the apartness of the object intended for display.

A stage empty of everything but a single chair would imply the kind of loneliness suitable for a Beckett-style monologue. This assumes, of course, that the chair is of the ordinary kind that usually exists in the company of other chairs like itself. A stage empty of everything save a pedestal is a shrine. We can imagine it a tomb. We can imagine it a place where Orestes and Electra encounter each other to plot their matricide under sanctified auspices. A room with a single chair is a habitation, but a lonely one. A room with only a pedestal is a sanctum, awaiting a visitation. The pedestal would be a marginal item in the household inventory, which requires the bed, the table, and some chairs. It implies two planes of being within the domus, one for objects of use and the other for objects defined by *presence.* This presence transfers to the pedestal itself. It is altogether appropriate for Castle to have said about *Constellation* (1989) that it has "good presence." We would expect nothing less of a pedestal.

It is thus appropriate that the Pedestal Pieces should carry, as Castle's pieces certainly do, implications of preciousness. For all its log-likeness, the base of *Cavalcade* (1989) seems to contain some precious substance, such as gold. Pedestals are carved of rare marbles or malachites, of stone that is either brilliantly colored and patterned, or white and pure, like alabaster. They will often carry a heavy, upward spiral, emphasizing the concept of ascent to the pedestal capital. Castle works within a rich tradition in carrying out the spiral motif; the base of *Constellation* seems like a miniature mountain around which a road curves to the pinnacle. That the pedestal should display virtuosity of carving or of workmanship fits magnificently with its meaning. After all, the singularity of the object to be poised atop the pedestal almost demands that the pedestal be a sacrifice of material things, that it should be rare and difficult and priceless.

It is true that the top form in *Black Gold* (1989) is a cabinet. At least it is hollowed out and has a door, but it is surely not a place for serious storage. Rather, it hides a sacred room in which the being for whom the pedestal exists should be housed. I was not surprised, but merely enlightened, when this sacred room was opened to reveal an effigy of Bart Simpson, an ephemeral godling. Peter Joseph, in whose offices the pedestal resides, explained that one really never knows what someone will have put in there, hence what one will find when one opens the door to the cabinet. This fits with the concept of the numinousness of the pedestal. One should open the door, as to an altarpiece, with a sense of awe, or at least of anticipation.

The top of *Black Gold* is sharply pointed, like a roof. This suggests even more strongly that the "cabinet" is a small temple. The edges are sloped to discourage placing anything on top of it, as if to say: Thou shalt have no other gods above me. Castle's motives, I think, are somewhat less arch. In his complex history of struggle with the idea of art, he was still finding it imperative, as late as 1989 or 1990, to subvert use. The bowl-like form that tops *Cavalcade* is level and smooth, so one could put something on it—except that Castle has there emplaced a brilliantly polished sphere. He explains: "The ball puts the piece in use and completes the picture. There's no bowl of fruit or vase of flowers necessary." The ball "completes the picture" in the sense that there is now a representation of the upper surface of a pedestal. It would be wrong, in violation of aesthetic canon, to invade the picture and treat the surface as though it were real. That is one reading. Another is that the ball itself emblemizes the being for whom the pedestal was made, or perhaps the ball holds the place for the exalted being, and insures that no unsuitable object, such as a bowl of fruit or a vase of flowers, should occupy it instead. (This overlooks the fact that fruits and flowers are standard forms of offerings, sacrifices rather than decorations.) The interpretation covers many of the Pedestal Pieces, the tops of which are either tipped, so as to be unable to hold objects; pointed; or preempted by other objects internal to the pieces, such as the ball.

Wendell Castle's motivation is doubtless less ritualized; he wants to rid the piece of the use that he still feels disfigures furniture, denying it arthood. I suspect that he holds the view that the Pedestal Pieces really are sculptures. Of *Constellation,* he says (I think hopefully, or at least wistfully), "It's big, it gets to be human size. I think of it a little bit like a figure."

We might, for a moment, pretend that these works *are* in fact mere sculptures. I wonder what I, as a critic, might think of them were they to be exhibited together and without any of the more obvious pieces of furniture. Perhaps I would say that here is an artist who has a vocabulary of modular pieces, which he arranges in different combinations and in conformity with a certain syntax. I would remark on the fact that there will be as few as two modules, but never more than four, and that the assemblages are somewhat monotonously vertical. I might wonder whether the ball was a kind of period, or the cone in *Constellation* or in *Reality Is Illusion* (1989) a kind of exclamation point—and I would perhaps think that this reading is confirmed in *Bright Rewards* (1989), where there is a cone atop a ball that really becomes an exclamation point. I would now see these works as sentences, placed vertically like sentences in Chinese, but with Western punctuation. Then I would begin to think about the virtuosity and the richness. I would wonder if the pieces were not metaphorically "golden words" (as on the tusk-like base of *Speaking Words of Wisdom,* where gold symbolizes the value of the words inscribed in helical lines around it). I would think of the sculptural pieces as texts, as writ, as religious script. I am not a formalist. I would not think in terms of things like balance and rhythm. I would look for meanings, and the meanings I would find in these sculptures would not differ so much from the meaning they take through their identity as pedestals. Their meaning as furniture that is art, however, is even greater and deeper than the meaning they might have were we to disinterpret them, and try to read them merely as sculpture.

The human figure, at least in the West, was for a very long time the central subject of sculpture. Sculpture showed ideal men and women, first as gods and goddesses, then as emperors and poets, and finally as sacred beings, such as martyrs, penitents, and virgins. All of these belong on top of pedestals. The pedestal itself belongs to the form of life the statue defines when construed as an object in which power resides; the pedestal is what communicates that power.

In recent years, sculptors have made a concerted effort to displace the pedestal. They have put their sculptures on the ground, as if to overcome the distance between them and ordinary humanity, a distance for which that between art and life was itself perhaps a kind of metaphor. To make pedestals today is to reaffirm the relationships that contemporary sculpture repudiates, and to celebrate the very distances and differences the erasure of the pedestal seeks to overcome. That is what these pieces would lose if they were not seen as pedestals, but were seen instead merely as sculptures composed of vertically staggered modules.

I have sought to articulate the transformative metaphor carried by the Pedestal Pieces of Wendell Castle, and to make explicit the meaning these pieces of furniture have when their identity as furniture is displayed rather than hidden. Even more universal than the meaning of the clothes we wear, the meaning of pieces of furniture condense human life as it is lived. The metaphors of furniture as art derive from these rich meanings, which are only grudgingly beginning to be reasserted or allowed. Furniture no longer needs to storm the dubious bastions of art by disguising itself as sculpture or some other thing; for it can be accepted as art in its own right, as the work of Wendell Castle so superbly shows.

Unless otherwise noted,

dimensions are in inches and in order of

height, width, and depth.

Angel Chairs

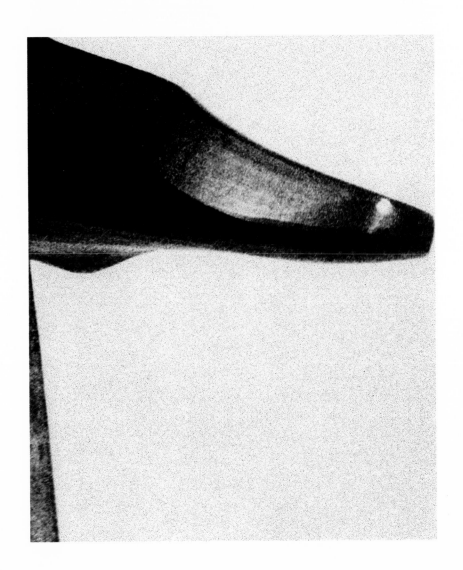

Angel of Blind Justice
1990
Stained mahogany, birdseye maple.
46 x 60 x 28

Living Spirits
1990
Stained mahogany, curly maple.
54 x 53 ¼ x 26 ½

Dark Secrets
1990
(Ladder-back Chair with Mountain)
Stained mahogany, birdseye maple, bubinga.
48 x 68 x 30
Collection of Sydney and Frances Lewis

True Dreams
1990
Stained and painted mahogany, curly maple.
57 ½ x 46 x 36
Collection of the Delaware Art Museum

Eternal Trust

1990

Stained mahogany, curly maple.

30 x 30 x 50

Harmonious Opportunities

1990

Stained and painted mahogany, avodire.

47 x 60 x 41

Neglected Affirmations
1990
Stained mahogany, satinwood, gold leaf.
40 X 54 X 43

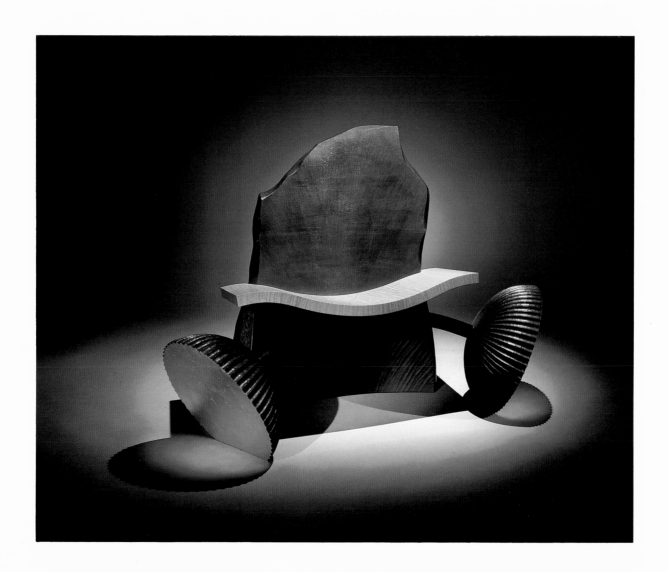

Singing Insights

1990

Stained and painted mahogany, satinwood.

49 x 40 x 27
49 x 46 x 27

Anticipated Risk
1990
Stained mahogany, Corian.
65 x 38 x 28

Bolstered Egos
1990
Stained mahogany, avodire, patined bronze.
32 ½ x 45 x 53 ½

Supported Affections
1990
Stained mahogany, curly maple, patined bronze.
37 ½ x 64 x 41

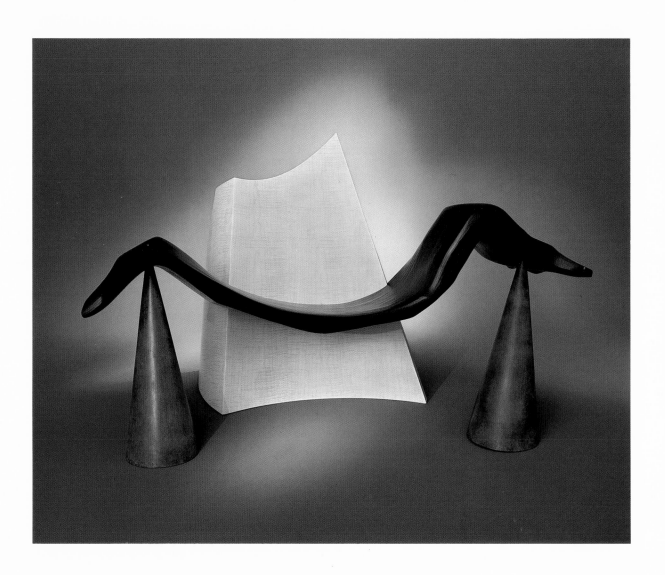

Liberated Egos
1990
Mahogany, avodire.
35 ½ x 46 x 53

Pedestal Pieces

Past Joys
1990
Patined bronze, stained mahogany, gold leaf.
63 x 20 diameter

Reality is Illusion

1989

Bleached mahogany, stained walnut,
patined bronze, gold leaf.

62 ½ x 22 x 22

Black Gold
1989
Stained mahogany, bleached lacewood, gold leaf.
68 ½ x 22 ½ x 18

Tip of a Thought
1989
Stained mahogany, gold leaf.
48 x 19 ½ x 22 ½

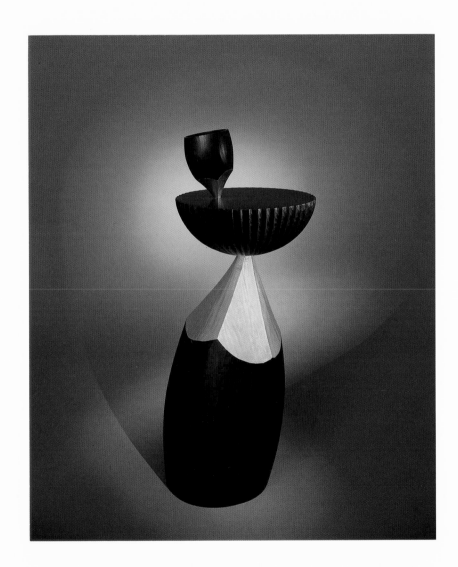

Into Reality
1989
Stained cherry, gold leaf.

37 X 30 X 22

Bright Rewards
1989
Stained mahogany, patined bronze, gold leaf.
66 ½ x 19 diameter

Cavalcade

1989
Stained mahogany, bleached lacewood,
patined copper, gold leaf.

48 ¼ x 24 x 17 ½

Constellation
1989
Stained mahogany, patined copper.
64 x 18 x 18

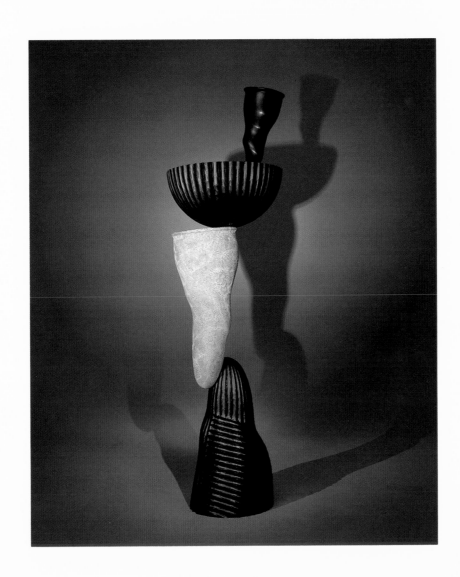

Altered Perception

1990

Stained aluminum, stained mahogany, gold leaf.

70 x 20 diameter

Alpha Choice

1989

Patined copper, stained mahogany, bleached lacewood.

58 x 20 x 20

Collection of Charles Dailey

Forbidden Passion
1990
Black granite, patined copper.
54 ¼ x 16 diameter

Fallow Desires

1990

Stained mahogany, patined copper.

48 x 24 ½ diameter

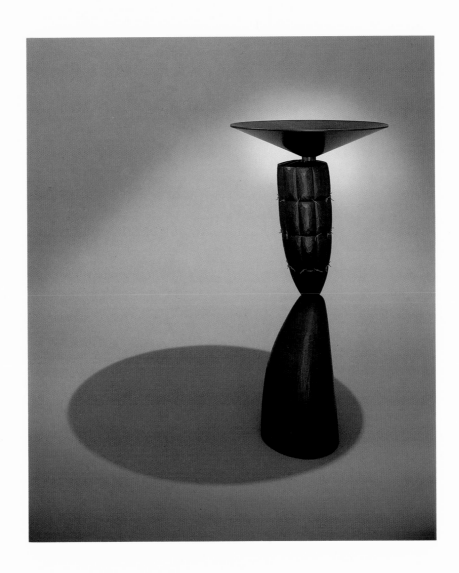

Common Ground
1989
Stained cherry, bleached lacewood,
patined copper, Plexiglas.

47 X 59 X 17

Mountain Works

I Know the Way
1990
Stained walnut, curly maple, ebony, patined brass.
42 ½ x 63 x 15 ½

Black Metamorphosis
1990
Stained mahogany, cocobola, patined bronze.
29 ½ x 89 x 57

Tuned Perception
1990
Lacewood, patined copper.
71 x 61 x 22

Time is Man's Angel

1990

Curly maple, patined copper,
aluminum, gold leaf, electric movement.

90 x 64 x 24

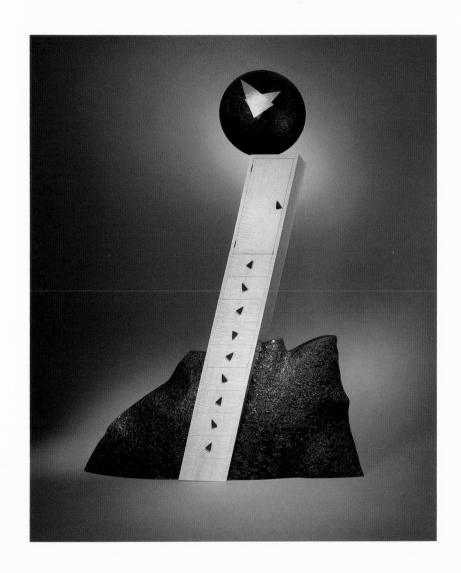

Deeper Reasons
1990
Stained mahogany, bubinga.
38 x 60 x 22

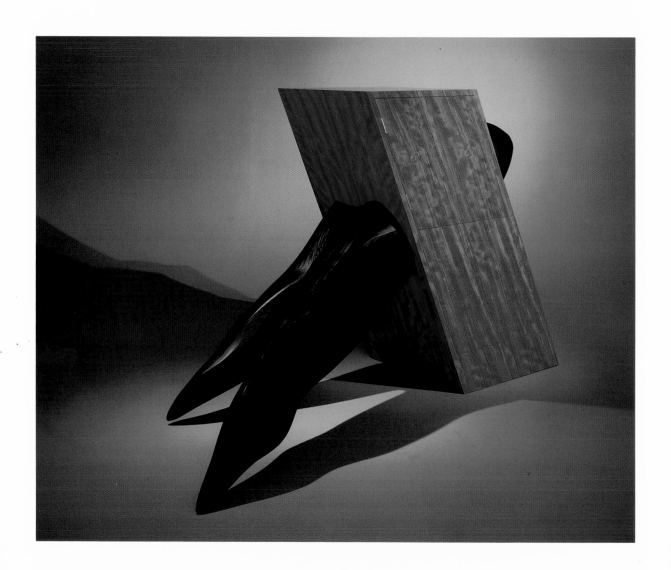

Diverse Works

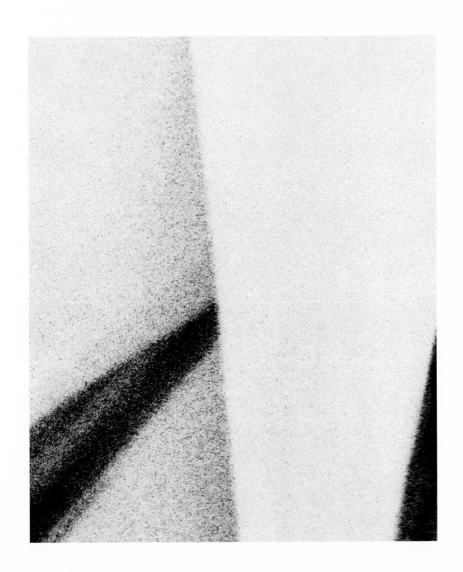

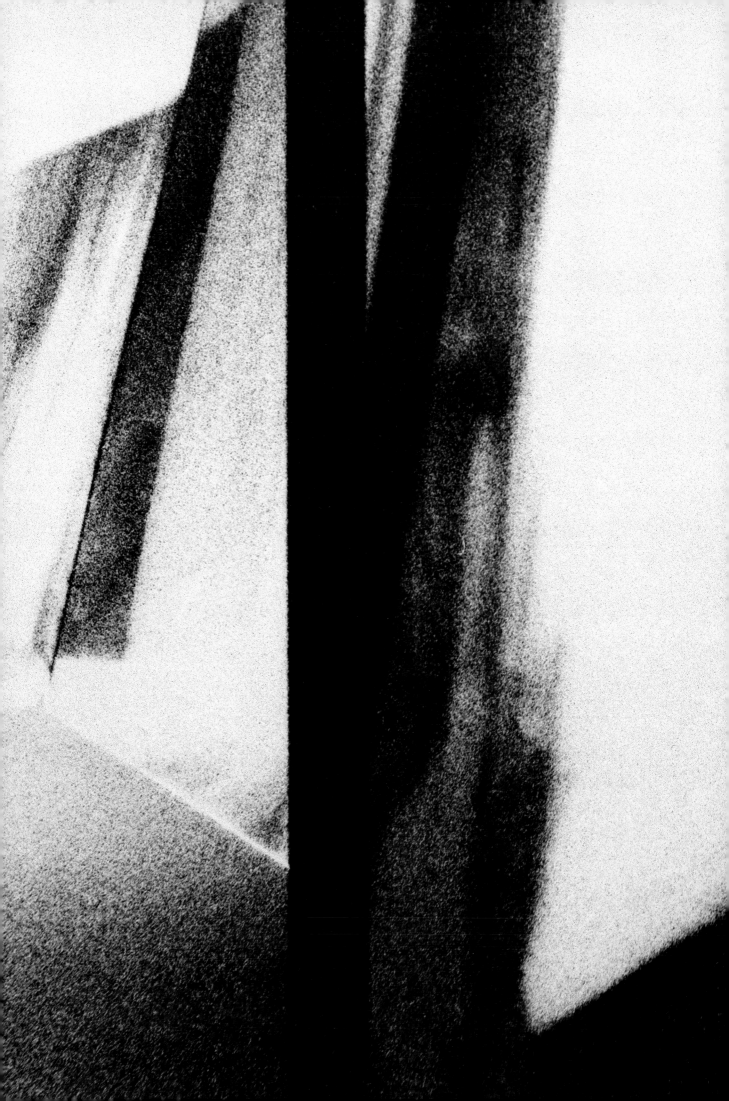

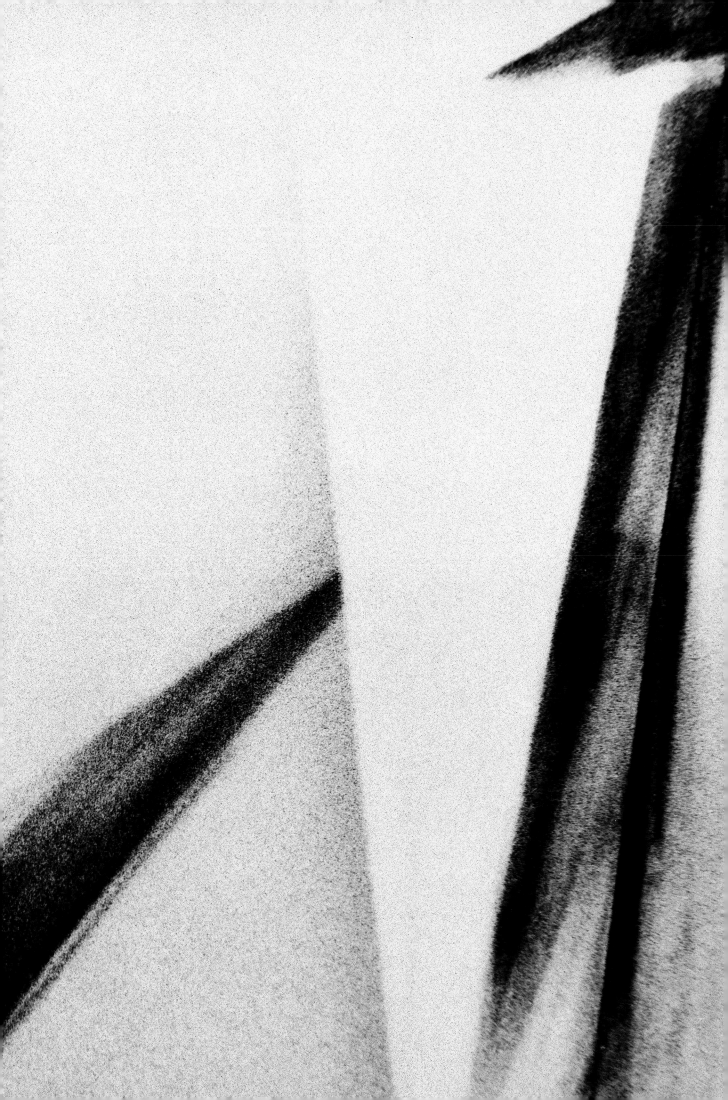

Speaking Words of Wisdom
1989
Stained mahogany, white gold leaf.
46 ½ x 29 x 24

Top of the World

1989

Bubinga, leather, painted and
stained cherry, gold leaf.

79 x 29 x 32

Presence

1990
Bleached maple, patined bronze and brass,
stained mahogany. Edition of 12.

24 X 15 X 10

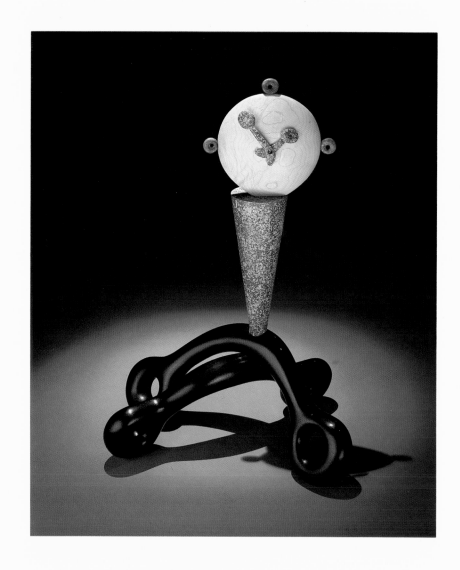

Mercury's Dream

1989

Painted mahogany, cast aluminum, curly sycamore,
pear, maple, electric movement.

61 ½ x 48 x 15

Ivory Spirit

1989

Curly sycamore, stained mahogany, maple,
Steinway & Sons Professional Upright.

Piano: 57 ¾ x 58 ¾ x 28 ¾
Stool: 19 x 34 ½ x 16

Bold Venture

1990

Bubinga, ebony, stained mahogany,
maple, aluminum, brass, leather,
Steinway & Sons Living Room Grand Piano.

Piano: 40 x 57 x 72
Stool: 19 x 34 ½ x 16

Whirlaway
1990
Bubinga, stained mahogany, stained red oak.
36 ½ x 86 x 33

Native Dancer
1990
Curly maple, stained mahogany.
16 x 43 x 32

Heard But Not Seen
1989
Italian poplar, gesso, aniline dye, acrylic paint.
84 x 107 x 24

Dr. Caligari's Mistress' Desk

1990
Ebony, mahogany, gesso, aniline dye,
acrylic paint, leather.

Desk: 34 ¾ x 76 ½ x 37
Chair: 30 x 22 x 22

Black Beauty
1990
Macassar ebony, stained mahogany, patined bronze.
51 x 45 x 32

On the Tip of My Tongue
1990
Madrone, stained mahogany, patined bronze.
52 x 66 x 18 (36 open)

It's Not Over Till It's Over
1990
Curly maple, bubinga, ebony, patined bronze.
76 x 91 x 123

Wendell Castle

1932
Born Emporia, Kansas

Education

1958
BFA Industrial Design, University of Kansas

1961
MFA Sculpture, University of Kansas

Honorary Trustee, Renwick Gallery, Smithsonian
Institution

Commissioner, National Museum of American Art

Member, Board of Managers, Memorial Art Gallery of
the University of Rochester

Academic Appointments

1984-present
Artist-in-Residence, Rochester Institute of Technology,
School for American Craftsmen

1980-1988
Wendell Castle School, Scottsville, NY

1969-1980
State University of New York, Brockport

1962-1969
Rochester Institute of Technology, School for American
Craftsmen

1959-1961
University of Kansas, Lawrence

Awards

1988
Visual Artists Fellowship Grant, National Endowment
for the Arts

1988
Golden Plate Award, American Academy of Achievement

1987
Honorary Doctor of Humane Letters, St. John Fisher
College, Rochester

1986
Fellowship, New York Foundation for the Arts

1986
Fellowship, American Craft Council

1979
Honorary Doctor of Fine Arts, Maryland Institute of
Art, Baltimore

1977
Lillian Fairchild Award, University of Rochester

1972
Louis Comfort Tiffany Foundation Grant

Collections and Commissions

Permanent Collections

Metropolitan Museum of Art, New York
Museum of Fine Arts, Boston
Museum of Fine Arts, Houston
Detroit Institute of Arts
The Brooklyn Museum
American Craft Museum, New York
Philadelphia Museum of Art
Museum of Art, St. Louis
Hunter Museum of Art, Chattanooga
The Art Institute of Chicago
Delaware Art Museum, Wilmington
Cincinnati Art Museum
Milwaukee Art Museum
Lannan Foundation Collection
Renwick Gallery, Smithsonian Institute
Memorial Art Galley, Rochester
Bevier Gallery, Rochester Institute of Technology
University of Utah Art Gallery, Salt Lake City
Ithaca College Art Museum
Everson Museum, Syracuse
Addison Gallery of American Art, Andover
Nordenfieldske Kunstindustrimuseet, Oslo, Norway
The Mobile Museum of Fine Arts

Selected Corporate and Private Collections

American Express Corporation
Johnson Wax
Sydney and Frances Lewis
John and Robin Stephenson
Sydney Bestoff III
Garry Knox Bennett
Ron Abramson
Penelope Hunter-Stiebel
Philippe de Montebello
The Forbes Magazine Collection
Simeon Bruner
Thomas Armstrong
Edward Margoulies
Martin Margulies
Jim Henson
Jennifer Johnson
Lee Nordness
Drs. Paul and Gloria Choi
Mr. and Mrs. Daniel Fendrick
Mr. and Mrs. Harvey Kaplan
Mr. and Mrs. Roger Berlind
Mr. and Mrs. VanBuren N. Hansford, Jr.
Edward Moultrop

Selected Commissions

Detroit Institute of Arts
Pillar Bryton Partners
Maccabees Mutual Life Insurance
Steinway & Sons
Hammerson Canada, Inc.
Cincinnati Art Museum
Daphne Farago
Charles and Mapes Stamm

III

Bibliography

Bayer, Patricia, ed. *The Fine Art of the Furniture Maker: Conversations with Wendell Castle, Artist, and Penelope Hunter-Stiebel, Curator, About Selected Works from the Metropolitan Museum of Art.* Rochester: Memorial Art Gallery of the University of Rochester, 1981.

Castle, Wendell, and David Edman. *The Wendell Castle Book of Wood Lamination.* New York: Van Nostrand Reinhold, Co., 1980.

Conway, Patricia. *Art for Everyday: The New Craft Movement.* New York: Clarkson Potter/Publishers, 1990.

Dormer, Peter. *The New Furniture: Trends and Traditions.* London: Thames and Hudson, 1987.

Giovannini, Joseph, Davira Taragin, and Edward S. Cooke, Jr. *Furniture by Wendell Castle.* New York: Hudson Hills Press, 1989.

Naeve, Milo M. *Identifying American Furniture: A Pictorial Guide to Styles and Terms Colonial to Contemporary.* New York: W.W. Norton & Company, 1989.

Stone, Michael A. *Contemporary American Woodworkers.* Salt Lake City: Gibbs M. Smith, 1986.